DIGITAL TELEVISION

Digital Television MPEG-1, MPEG-2 and principles of the DVB system

Hervé Benoit

A member of the Hodder Headline Group
LONDON • SYDNEY • AUCKLAND
Copublished in North, South and Central America by
John Wiley & Sons Inc., New York • Toronto

First published in Great Britain in 1997 by Arnold,
a member of the Hodder Headline Group,
338 Euston Road, London NW1 3BH

This book is adapted and translated by the author from Benoit, H., 1996:
*La Télévision Numérique: MPEG-1, MPEG-2, et les principes du système
européen DVB*. Paris: Dunod.

Copublished in North, Central and South America by
John Wiley & Sons, Inc., 605 Third Avenue,
New York, NY 10158–0012

Whilst the advice and information in this book is believed to be true and
accurate at the date of going to press, neither the author nor the publisher
can accept any legal responsibility or liability for any errors or omissions
that may be made.

British Library Cataloguing in Publication Data
A catalogue record for this book is available from the British Library

Library of Congress Cataloging-in-Publication Data
A catalog record for this book is available from the Library of Congress

ISBN 0 340 69190 5
ISBN 0 471 23810 4

3 4 5 6 7 8 9 10

Typeset in 11/12pt Times by J&L Composition Ltd, Filey, North Yorkshire
Printed and bound in Great Britain by J W Arrowsmith Ltd, Bristol

Contents

Foreword

This book does not aim to make the reader an expert in digital television (which the author himself is not). Rather, its purpose is to describe and explain, as simply and as completely as possible, the various aspects of the very complex problems that had to be solved in order to define reliable standards for broadcasting digital pictures to the consumer, and the solutions chosen for the European **DVB** system (Digital Video Broadcasting) based on the international **MPEG-2** compression standard.

The book is intended for readers with a background in electronics and some knowledge of conventional analogue television (a reminder of the basic principles of existing television standards is presented for those who require it) and for those with a basic digital background. The main goal is to enable readers to understand the principles of this new technology, to have a relatively global perspective on it, and, if they wish, to investigate further any particular aspect by reading more specialized and more detailed books. At the end, there is a short bibliography and a glossary of abbreviations and expressions, which will help readers to access some of these references.

For ease of understanding, after a general presentation of the problem, the order in which the main aspects of digital television broadcast standards are described follows the logical progression of the signal processing steps on the transmitter side – from raw digitization used in TV studios to **source coding** (MPEG-2 compression and multiplexing), and on to **channel coding** (from forward error correction to RF modulation). **JPEG** and **MPEG-1** 'predecessor' standards of MPEG-2 are also described, as MPEG-2 uses the same basic principles.

The book ends with a functional description of a digital **IRD** (integrated receiver decoder), or **set-top box**, which the concepts discussed in preceding chapters will help to demystify, and with a discussion of future prospects.

H Benoit
1997

Acknowledgements

I would like to thank all those who lent their support in the realization of this book, especially:

- Loïc Potier and Issa Rakhodai for their advice and the documents they supplied;

- Robbert Van Der Wal and his team for their training and for many of the figures illustrating this book;

- Achim Ibenthal, Allen Light, the DVB Project Office, the EBU Technical Publication Service and the ETSI Infocentre for permission to reproduce the figures which they provided.

I am also very grateful to my wife Rosemarie and daughter Elsa for their sympathy during all the time taken by the writing of this book.

Introduction

Only 10 years ago, in the mid-1980s, the possibility of broadcasting fully digital pictures to the consumer was still seen as a faraway prospect, and one that was definitely not technically or economically realistic before the turn of the century. The main reason for this was the very high bit-rate required for the transmission of digitized 525- or 625-line live video pictures (from 108 to 270 Mb/s without compression). Another reason was that, at that time, it seemed more urgent and important – at least in the eyes of some politicians and technocrats – to improve the quality of the TV picture, and huge amounts of money were invested by the three main world players (first Japan, then Europe, and finally the USA) in order to develop Improved Definition TeleVision (**IDTV**) and High Definition TeleVision systems (**HDTV**), with vertical resolutions from 750 lines for IDTV to 1125 or 1250 lines for HDTV.

Simply digitized, HDTV pictures would have required bit-rates that were four times higher than 'conventional' pictures, of the order of up to one gigabit per second! This is why most of the HDTV proposals (**MUSE** in Japan, **HD-MAC** in Europe, and the first American HD proposals) were at that time defined as analogue systems with a digital assistance which can be seen as a prelude to fully digital compression.

However, by the beginning of the 1990s, the situation had completely changed. Very quick development of efficient compression algorithms, resulting in, among other things, the JPEG standard for fixed images and later the MPEG standard for moving pictures, showed the possibility to reduce drastically the amount of data required for the transmission of digital pictures (bit-rates from 1.5 to 30 Mb/s depending on the resolution chosen and the picture content).

At the same time, continuous progress in IC technology allowed the realization, at an affordable price, of the complex chips and associated memory required for decompression of the digital pictures. In addition, it appeared that the price of a HDTV receiver would not quickly reach a level affordable by most consumers, not so much due to the electronics cost, but mainly because of the very high cost of the display, regardless of the technology used (big 16/9 tube, LCD projector or any other known technology). Furthermore, most consumers seemed more interested in the content and the number of programmes offered than in an improvement in the picture quality, and economic crises in most countries resulted in a demand for 'brown goods' oriented more towards the cheaper end of the market.

Mainly on the initiative of the US industry, which could take advantage of its traditional predominance in digital data processing to regain influence in the electronic consumer goods market, studies have been reoriented towards the definition of systems allowing diffusion of digital pictures with equivalent or slightly better quality than current analogue standards, but with many other features made possible by complete digitization of the signal. The first digital TV broadcasting for the consumer started in mid-1994 with the 'DirecTV' project, and its success was immediate, resulting in more than one million subscribers after one year.

However, the Europeans had not gone to sleep – they decided at the end of 1991 to stop working on analogue HDTV (HD-MAC), and created the European Launching Group (**ELG**) in order to define and standardize a digital TV broadcasting system. This gave birth in 1993 to the **DVB** project (Digital Video Broadcasting), based on the 'main profile at main level' (**MP@ML**) of the international MPEG-2 compression standard.

MPEG-2 is downwards compatible with MPEG-1 and has provisions for a compatible evolution towards HDTV by using higher levels and profiles. This resulted in the standardization of three variants for the various transmission media – satellite (DVB-S), cable (DVB-C) and terrestrial (DVB-T) – which occurred between 1994 and 1996.

1 Colour television: a review of current standards

Let us begin with a bit of history . . .

1.1 Monochrome TV basics

It should be borne in mind that all current TV standards in use today are derived from the 'black and white' TV standards started in the 1940s and '50s, which have defined their framework.

The first attempts at electromechanical television began at the end of the 1920s, using the Nipkow disk for analysis and reproduction of the scene to be televised, with a definition of 30 lines and 12.5 images per second. This low definition resulted in a video bandwidth of less than 10 KHz, allowing these pictures to be broadcast on an ordinary AM/MW or LW transmitter. The resolution soon improved to 60, 90 and 120 lines and then stabilized for a while on 180 lines (Germany, France) or 240 lines (England, USA) around 1935. Scanning was '**progressive**', which meant that all lines of the pictures were scanned sequentially in one **frame**, as depicted in Fig. 1.1 (numbered here for a 625 line system).

These definitions, used for the first 'regular' broadcasts, were the practical limit for the Nipkow disk used for picture analysis; the cathode ray tube (CRT) started to be used for display at the receiver side. In order to avoid disturbances due to electromagnetic radiation from transformers or a ripple in the power supply, the picture rate (or frame rate) was derived from the mains

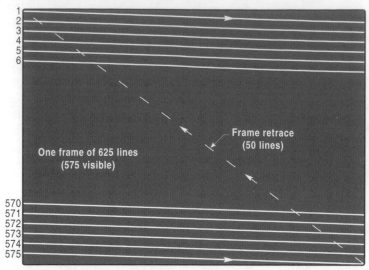

Fig. 1.1 Schematic representation of progressive scanning

frequency. This resulted in refresh rates of 25 pictures/s in Europe and 30 pictures/s in the USA. The bandwidth required was of the order of 1 MHz, which implied the use of VHF frequencies (in the order of 40–50 MHz) for transmission. However, the spatial resolution of these first TV pictures was still insufficient, and they were affected by a very annoying **flicker** due to the fact that their refresh rate was too low.

During the years just preceding World War II, image analysis had become fully electronic with the invention of the iconoscope, and definitions in use attained 405 lines (England) to 441 lines (USA, Germany) or 455 lines (France), thanks to the use of **interlaced scanning**. This ingenious method, invented in 1927, consisted of scanning a first field made of the odd lines of the frame and then a second field made of the even lines (see Fig. 1.2), allowing the picture refresh rate for a given vertical resolution to be doubled (50 or 60 Hz instead of 25 or 30 Hz) without increasing the bandwidth required for broadcasting.

The need to maintain a link between picture rate and mains frequency, however, inevitably led to different standards on both sides of the Atlantic, even when the number of lines was identical (as in the case of the 441 line US and German systems). Nevertheless, these systems shared the following common features:

- a unique **composite** picture signal combining video, blanking and synchronization information (abbreviated to **VBS**, also described as video baseband signal; see Fig. 1.3);

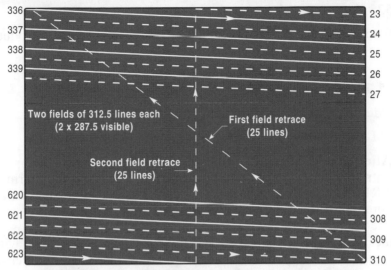

Fig. 1.2 Schematic representation of interlaced scanning (625 lines)

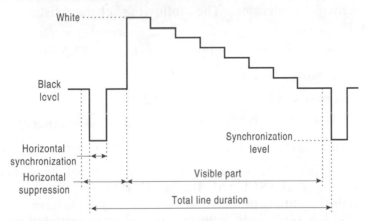

Fig. 1.3 View of a line of a composite monochrome video signal

- an interlaced scanning (order 2), recognized as the best compromise between flicker and the required bandwidth.

Soon afterwards, due to the increase in the size of the picture tube, and taking into account the eye's resolution in normal viewing conditions, the spatial resolution of these systems still appeared insufficient, and most experts proposed a vertical definition of between 500 and 700 lines. The following characteristics were finally chosen in 1941 for the US monochrome system, which later became **NTSC** when it was upgraded to colour in 1952:

- 525 lines, interlaced scanning (two fields of 262.5 lines);
- field frequency, 60 Hz (changed to 59.94 Hz upon the introduction of colour; see Note 1.1);
- line frequency, 15 750 Hz (60 × 262.5); later changed to 15 734 Hz with colour (59.94 × 262.5);
- video bandwidth, 4.2 MHz; negative video modulation;
- FM sound with carrier 4.5 MHz above the picture carrier.

After World War II, from 1949 onwards, most European countries (except France and Great Britain) adopted the German 'GERBER' standard, also known as **CCIR**. It can be seen as an adaptation of the US system to a 50 Hz field frequency, keeping a line frequency as near as possible to 15 750 Hz; this allowed some advantage to be taken of the American experience with receiver technology. This choice implied an increased number of lines (approximately in the ratio 60/50) and, consequently, a wider bandwidth in order to obtain well balanced horizontal and vertical resolutions. The following characteristics were defined:

- 625 lines, interlaced scanning (two fields of 312.5 lines)
- field frequency, 50 Hz
- line frequency, 15 625 Hz (50 × 312.5)
- video bandwidth, 5.0 MHz; negative video modulation
- FM sound carrier 5.5 MHz above the picture carrier.

This has formed the basis of all the European colour standards defined later (**PAL, SECAM, D2-MAC, PAL+**).

Until the beginning of the 1980s, different systems have been in use in the UK (405 lines, launched in 1937 and restarted after a long interruption during the war) and in France (819 lines, launched in 1949 by Henri de France, who also invented the SECAM system in 1957). These systems were not adapted to colour TV for consumer broadcasting due to the near impossibility of colour standard conversion with the technical means available at that time, and were finally abandoned after a period of **simulcast** with the new colour standard.

1.2 Black and white compatible colour systems

As early as the late 1940s, US TV set manufacturers and broadcasting companies competed in order to define the specifications of a colour TV system. The proposal officially approved in 1952 by the **FCC** (Federal Communications Commission), known as NTSC (National Television Standard Committee), was the RCA proposal. It was the only one built on the basis of bi-directional *compatibility* with the existing monochrome standard. A monochrome receiver was able to display the new colour broadcasts in black and white, and a colour receiver could, in the same way, display the existing black and white broadcasts, which comprised the vast majority of transmissions until the mid-1960s.

In Europe, official colour broadcasts started more than 10 years later, in 1967, with SECAM (séquentiel couleur à mémoire) and PAL (phase alternating line) systems.

Extensive preliminary studies on colour perception and a great deal of ingenuity were required to define these standards which, despite their imperfections, still satisfy most of the end users more than 40 years after the first of them, NTSC, came into being. The triple red/green/blue (RGB) signals delivered by the TV camera had to be transformed into a signal which, on the one hand, could be displayable without major artefacts on current black and white receivers, and on the other hand could be transmitted in the bandwidth of an existing TV channel – definitely not a simple task.

The basic idea was to transform, by a linear combination, the three (R, G, B) signals into three other equivalent **components**, Y, C_b, C_r (or Y, U, V):

$$Y = 0.587\ G + 0.299\ R + 0.114\ B \text{ is called the } \textit{luminance} \text{ signal}$$
$$C_b = 0.564\ (B - Y) \quad \text{or} \quad U = 0.493\ (B - Y) \text{ is called the } \textit{blue}$$
$$\textit{chrominance} \text{ or colour difference}$$
$$C_r = 0.713\ (R - Y) \quad \text{or} \quad V = 0.877\ (R - Y) \text{ is called the}$$
$$\textit{red chrominance} \text{ or colour difference}$$

The combination used for the luminance (or 'luma') signal has been chosen to be as similar as possible to the output signal of a monochrome camera, which allows the black and white receiver to treat it as a normal monochrome signal. The two chrominance (or 'chroma') signals represent the 'coloration' of the monochrome picture carried by the Y signal, and allow, by linear recombination with Y, the retrieval of the original RGB signals in the colour receiver.

Studies on visual perception have shown that the human eye's resolution is less acute for colour than for luminance transients. This means, for natural pictures at least, that chrominance signals can tolerate a strongly reduced bandwidth (one-half to one-quarter of the luminance bandwidth), which will prove very useful for putting the chrominance signals within the existing video spectrum. The Y, C_b, C_r combination is the common point to all colour TV systems, including the newest digital standards, which seems to prove that the choices of the colour TV pioneers were not so bad!

In order to be able to transport these three signals in an existing TV channel (6 MHz in the USA, 7 or 8 MHz in Europe), a subcarrier was added within the video spectrum, modulated by the reduced bandwidth chrominance signals, thus giving a new composite signal called the **CVBS** (Colour Video Baseband Signal; see Fig. 1.4). In order not to disturb the luminance and the black and white receivers, this carrier had to be placed in the highest part of the video spectrum and had to stay within the limits of the existing video bandwidth (4.2 MHz in the USA, 5–6 MHz in Europe; see Fig. 1.5).

Up to this point, no major differences between the three world standards (NTSC, PAL, SECAM) have been highlighted. The differences that do exist mainly concern the way of modulating this subcarrier and its frequency.

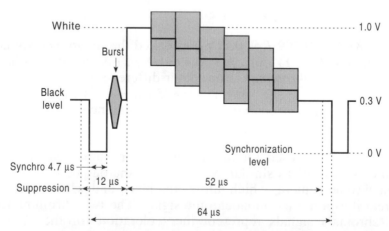

Fig. 1.4 View of a line of composite colour video signal (PAL or NTSC)

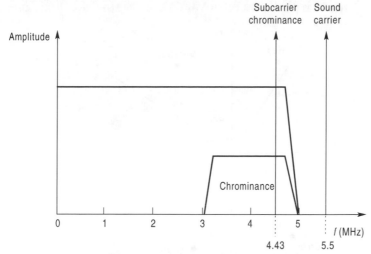

Fig. 1.5 Frequency spectrum of the PAL signal

1.2.1 NTSC

This system uses a **line-locked** subcarrier at 3.579 545 MHz (= 455 × F_h/2), amplitude modulated with a suppressed carrier following two orthogonal axes (quadrature amplitude modulation, or **QAM**), by two signals, **I** (in phase) and **Q** (quadrature), carrying the chrominance information. These signals are two linear combinations of $R - Y$ and $B - Y$, corresponding to a 33° rotation of the vectors relative to the $B - Y$ axis. This process results in a vector (Fig. 1.6), the phase of which represents the tint, and the amplitude of which represents colour intensity (saturation).

A reference burst at 3.579 545 MHz with a 180° phase relative to the $B - Y$ axis superimposed on the back porch allows the receiver to rebuild the subcarrier required to demodulate I and Q signals. The choice for the subcarrier of an odd multiple of half the line frequency is such that the luminance spectrum (made up of discrete stripes centred on multiples of the line frequency) and the chrominance spectrum (discrete stripes centred on odd multiples of half the line frequency) are interlaced, making an almost perfect separation theoretically possible by the use of **comb filters** in the receiver.

Practice, however, soon showed that NTSC was very sensitive to phase rotations introduced by the transmission channel, which resulted in very important tint errors, especially in the region of flesh tones (thus leading to the necessity of a tint correction button accessible to the user on the receivers and to the famous 'never

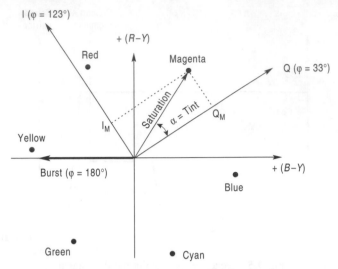

Fig. 1.6 Colour plan of the NTSC system

twice the same colour' expression). This led Europeans to look for solutions to this problem, which resulted in the SECAM and PAL systems.

1.2.2   SECAM

This standard eliminates the main drawback of the NTSC system by using frequency modulation for the subcarrier, which is insensitive to phase rotations; however, FM does not allow simultaneous modulation of the subcarrier by two signals, as does QAM.

The clever means of circumventing this problem consisted of considering that the colour information of two consecutive lines was sufficiently similar to be considered as identical. This reduces chroma resolution by a factor of 2 in the vertical direction, making it more consistent with the horizontal resolution resulting from bandwidth reduction of the chroma signals. Therefore, it is possible to transmit alternately one chrominance component, $D'_b = 1.5(B - Y)$, on one line and the other, $D'_r = - 1.9(R - Y)$, on the next line. It is then up to the receiver to recover the two D'_b and D'_r signals simultaneously, which can be done by means of a 64 μs delay line (one line duration) and a permutator circuit. Subcarrier frequencies chosen are 4.250 MHz (= 272 × F_h) for the line carrying D'_b and 4.406 250 MHz (= 282 × F_h) for D'_r.

This system is very robust, and gives a very accurate tint reproduction, but it has some drawbacks due to the frequency modulation – the subcarrier is always present, even in non-coloured parts of the pictures, making it more visible than in NTSC or PAL on black and white, and the continuous nature of the FM spectrum does not allow an efficient comb filtering; rendition of sharp transients between highly saturated colours is not optimum due to the necessary truncation of maximum FM deviation. In addition, direct mixing of two or more SECAM signals is not possible.

1.2.3 PAL

This is a close relative of the NTSC system, whose main drawback it corrects. It uses a line-locked subcarrier at 4.433 619 MHz (= 1135/4 + 1/625 × F_h), which is QAM modulated by the two colour difference signals $U = 0.493$ $(B - Y)$ and $V = 0.877$ $(R - Y)$.

In order to avoid drawbacks due to phase rotations, the phase of the V carrier is inverted every second line, which allows cancellation of phase rotations in the receiver by adding the V signal from two consecutive lines by means of a 64 μs delay line (using the same assumption as in SECAM, that two consecutive lines can be considered as identical). In order to synchronize the V demodulator, the phase of the reference burst is alternated from line to line between +135° and −135° compared to the U vector (0°).

Other features of PAL are very similar to NTSC. In addition to the main PAL standard (sometimes called PAL B/G), there are two other less well known variants used in South America in order to accommodate the 6 MHz channels taken from NTSC:

- PAL M used in Brazil (525 lines/59.94 Hz, subcarrier at 3.575 611 MHz)

- PAL N used in Argentina (625 lines/50 Hz, subcarrier at 3.582 056 MHz).

1.2.4 MAC (multiplexed analogue components)

During the 1980s, Europeans attempted to define a common standard for satellite broadcasts, with the goal of improving picture and sound quality by eliminating drawbacks of composite systems (cross-colour, cross-luminance, reduced bandwidth) and by using digital sound. This resulted in the MAC systems, with a compatible extension towards HDTV (called HD-MAC).

D2-MAC is the most well known of these hybrid systems, even if it did not achieve its expected success, due to its late introduction and an earlier development of digital TV than anticipated. It replaces frequency division multiplexing of luminance, chrominance and sound (bandwidth sharing) of composite standards by a time division multiplexing (time sharing). It is designed to be compatible with normal (4/3) and wide screen (16/9) formats and can be considered in some aspects as an intermediate step on the route to all-digital TV signal transmission.

On the transmitter side, after sampling (Note 1.2) and analogue-to-digital conversion, Y, C_b and C_r signals are time-compressed by a factor of 2/3 for Y and 1/3 for C_b and C_r, scrambled if required, and then reconverted into analogue form in order to be transmitted sequentially over one line duration (see Fig. 1.7 illustrating one line of a D2-MAC signal). The part of the line usually occupied by synchronization and blanking is replaced by a burst of so-called duobinary data (hence the 'D2' in D2-MAC). These data carry the digital sound, synchronization and other information such as teletext, captioning and picture format (4/3 or 16/9), and in addition, for pay TV programmes, they carry the access control messages of the Eurocrypt system used with D2-MAC.

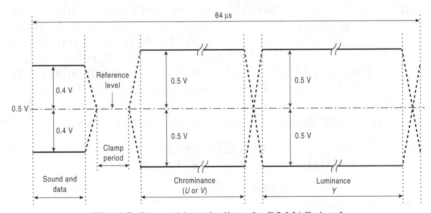

Fig. 1.7 Composition of a line of a D2-MAC signal

As in SECAM, C_b and C_r chroma components are transmitted alternately from line to line in order to reduce the necessary bandwidth and obtain equivalent resolutions along the two axes of the picture for the chrominance. This resolution corresponds to the so-called 4:2:0 format (see Section 2.2.2, p. 19); it is almost equivalent to the professional 4:2:2 format used in TV studios. Time division multiplexing results in the total elimination of cross-colour and cross-luminance effects, and in a luminance bandwidth of 5 MHz, a substantial improvement compared with PAL or SECAM.

1.2.5   PAL+

This is a recent development, the primary objective of which was to allow terrestrial transmission of improved definition 16/9 pictures (on appropriate receivers) in a compatible way with existing 4/3 PAL receivers (Note 1.3). To do this, the PAL+ encoder transforms the 576 useful lines of a 16/9 picture into a 4/3 picture in **letterbox** format (a format often used for the transmission of films on TV, with two horizontal black stripes above and below the picture). The visible part occupies only 432 lines (576 × 3/4) on a 4/3 receiver, and additional information for the PAL+ receiver is encoded in the remaining 144 lines.

The 432 line letterbox picture is obtained by vertical low-pass filtering of the original 576 lines, and the complementary high-pass filtering is transmitted on the 4.43 MHz subcarrier during the 144 black lines, which permits the PAL+ receiver to reconstruct a full-screen 16/9 high resolution picture.

In order to obtain the maximum bandwidth for luminance (5 MHz) and to reduce cross-colour and cross-luminance, the phase of the subcarrier of the two interlaced lines of consecutive fields is reversed. This process, known as 'colorplus', allows (by means of a frame memory in the receiver) cancellation of cross-luminance by adding the high part of the spectrum of two consecutive frames, and reduction of cross-colour by subtracting them.

A movement compensation is required to avoid artefacts introduced by the colorplus process on fast moving objects, which, added to the need for a frame memory, contributes to the relatively high cost of current PAL+ receivers. The PAL+ system results in a subjective quality equivalent to D2-MAC on a 16/9 receiver in good reception conditions (high signal/noise ratio).

In order to inform the receiver of the format of the programme being broadcast (4/3 or 16/9), signalling bits (**WSS**: wide screen signalling) and additional information (sound mode, etc.) are added to the first half of line 23 (Fig. 1.8), which permits the receiver to adapt its display format. The WSS signal can also be used by ordinary PAL 16/9 receivers simply to modify the vertical amplitude according to the format, which is sometimes referred to as the 'poor man's PAL+'.

After this introduction (hopefully not too lengthy), we will now attempt to describe as simply as possible the principles which have allowed the establishment of new all-digital television standards and services, the impact of which is still difficult to comprehend.

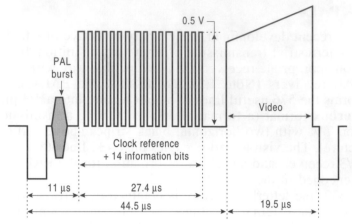

Fig. 1.8 View of line 23 of a PAL+ signal (WSS bits)

Note 1.1

This slight change in line and field frequencies was introduced in order to minimize the visual effect of beat frequency between sound (4.50 MHz) and colour (3.58 MHz) subcarriers in the receiver. This change was done by using the sound intercarrier as a reference for the line frequency

$$(15\ 734 = 4\ 500\ 000\ /286).$$

Note 1.2

D2-MAC is based on the 4:2:0 digital format (720 points/line for Y and 360 for C_b and C_r), but for practical reasons, these numbers had to be slightly reduced to 700 and 350, respectively. This is due to the fact that the duration of 720 samples at 13.5 MHz (53.33 µs) is more than the useful part of the analogue video line (52 µs), which could disturb clamping circuits in the receiver.

Note 1.3

PAL+ development took place between 1990 and 1992; after a period of experimental transmissions, official broadcasts started in Germany and other countries after the international 1995 Berlin radio/TV exhibition (IFA). PAL+ is officially adopted by most countries currently using the PAL system. The WSS format signalling information will also be used independently of PAL+ for conventional PAL or SECAM transmissions.

2 Digitization of video signals

2.1 Why digitize video signals?

For a number of years, video professionals at television studios have been using various digital formats, such as **D1** (components) and **D2** (composite), for recording and editing video signals. In order to ease the interoperability of equipment and international programme exchange, the former CCIR (Comité Consultatif International des Radiocommuncations; Note 2.1) has standardized conditions of digitization (recommendation CCIR-601) and interfacing (recommendation CCIR-656) of digital video signals in component form (Y, C_r, C_b in 4:2:2 format).

The main advantages of these digital formats are that they allow multiple copies to be made without any degradation in quality, and the creation of special effects not otherwise possible in analogue format, and they simplify editing of all kinds, as well as permitting international exchange independent of the broadcast standard to be used for diffusion (NTSC, PAL, SECAM, D2-MAC, MPEG). However, the drawback is the very important bit-rate, which makes these formats unsuitable for transmission to the end user without prior signal compression.

2.2 Digitization formats

If one wants to digitize an analogue signal of bandwidth F_{max}, it is necessary to sample its value with a sampling frequency F_s of at least twice the maximum frequency of this signal to keep its

integrity (Shannon sampling theorem). This is to avoid the negative **aliasing** effects of spectrum fall-back: in effect, sampling a
signal creates two parasitic sidebands above and below the sampling frequency, which range from $F_s - F_{max}$ to $F_s + F_{max}$, as well
as around harmomics of the sampling frequency (Fig. 2.1).

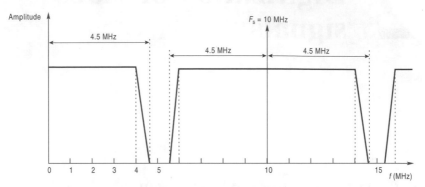

Fig. 2.1 Spectrum of a sampled signal (when $F_s > 2 \times F_{max}$)

In order to avoid mixing of the input signal spectrum and the
lower part of the first parasitic sideband, the necessary and sufficient condition is that $F_s - F_{max} > F_{max}$, which is realized if $F_s > 2$
F_{max}. This means that the signal to be digitized needs to be
efficiently filtered in order to ensure that its bandwidth does not
exceed $F_{max} = F_s/2$.

For component video signals from a studio source, which can
have a bandwidth of up to 6 MHz, the CCIR prescribes a sampling
frequency of $F_s = 13.5$ MHz locked on the line frequency (Note
2.2). This frequency is independent of the scanning standard, and
represents $864 \times F_h$ for 625 line systems and $858 \times F_h$ for 525
line systems. The number of active samples per line is 720 in both
cases. In such a line-locked sampling system, samples are at the
same fixed place on all lines in a frame, and also from frame to
frame, and so are situated on a rectangular grid. For this reason,
this sampling method is called **orthogonal sampling** (Fig. 2.2), as
opposed to other sampling schemes used for composite video
sampling ($4 \times F_{sc}$ subcarrier locked sampling for instance).

The most economic method in terms of bit-rate for video signal
digitization seems, *a priori*, to be to use the composite signal as a
source; however, the quality will be limited by its composite
nature. Taking into account the fact that 8 bits (corresponding
to 256 **quantization** steps) is the minimum required for a good
signal to quantization noise ratio ($S_v/N_q \cong 59$ dB; Note 2.3), the

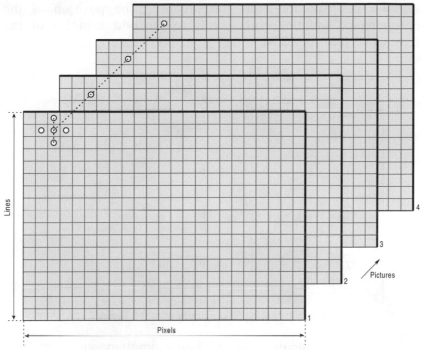

Fig. 2.2 Orthogonal sampling structure of a picture

bit-rate required by this composite digitization is 13.5 × 8 = 108 Mb/s, which is already a lot!

However, digitization of a composite signal has little advantage over its analogue form for production purposes (practically the only one is the possibility of multiple copies without degradation). This is why this is not the preferred method for source signal digitization in broadcast applications, as the composite signal is not very suitable for most signal manipulations (editing, compression) or international exchanges.

2.2.1   The 4:2:2 format

Recommendation **CCIR-601**, established in 1982, defines digitization parameters for video signals in component form based on a Y C_b C_r signal in 4:2:2 format (four Y samples for two C_b samples and two C_r samples) with 8 bits per sample (with a provision for extension to 10 bits per sample). The sampling frequency is 13.5 MHz for luminance and 6.75 MHz for chrominance, regardless of the standard of the input signal. This results in 720 active video samples per line for luminance, and 360 active samples per line for each chrominance. The position of the chrominance samples corresponds to the odd samples of the luminance (see Fig. 2.3).

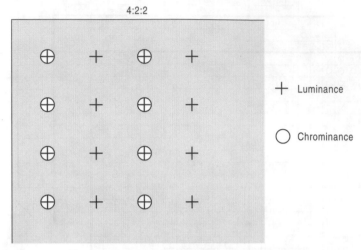

Fig. 2.3 Position of samples in the 4:2:2 format

Chrominance signals C_r and C_b being simultaneously available at every line, vertical resolution for chrominance is the same as for luminance (480 lines for 525 line systems, 576 lines for 625 line systems). The total bit-rate resulting from this process is $13.5 \times 8 + 2 \times 6.75 \times 8 = 216$ Mb/s. With a quantization on 10 bits, the bit-rate becomes 270 Mb/s! However, if one takes into account the redundancy involved in digitizing the inactive part of the video signal (horizontal and vertical blanking periods), the useful bit-rate goes down to 166 Mb/s with 8 bits per sample. These horizontal and vertical blanking periods can be filled by other useful data, such as digital sound, sync and other information.

Recommendation **CCIR-656** defines standardized electrical interfacing conditions for 4:2:2 signals digitized according to recommendation CCIR-601. This is the format used for interfacing D1 digital video recorders, and is therefore sometimes referred to as the *D1 format*.

The parallel version of this recommendation provides the signal in a multiplexed form (C_{r1} Y_1 C_{b1} Y_2 C_{r3} Y_3 C_{b3} . . .) on an 8-bit parallel interface, together with a 27 MHz clock (one clock period per sample). Synchronization and other data are included in the data flow. The normalized connector is a DB25 plug.

There is also a serial form of the CCIR-656 interface for

transmission on a 75 Ω coaxial cable with BNC connectors, requiring a slightly higher bit-rate (243 Mb/s) due to the use of 9 bits per sample in this mode.

2.2.2   4:2:0, SIF, CIF and QCIF formats

For applications that are less demanding in terms of resolution, and in view of the bit-rate reduction, a certain number of *by-products* of the 4:2:2 format have been defined, as follows.

The 4:2:0 format

This format is obtained from the 4:2:2 format by using the same chroma samples for two successive lines, in order to reduce the amount of memory required in processing circuitry while at the same time giving a vertical resolution of the same order as the horizontal resolution. Luminance and horizontal chrominance resolutions are the same as for the 4:2:2 format, and thus

- luminance resolution: 720 × 576 (625 lines) or 720 × 480 (525 lines)

- chrominance resolution: 360 × 288 (625 lines) or 360 × 240 (525 lines).

Figure 2.4 shows the position of chroma samples in the 4:2:0 format.

In order to avoid the chrominance line flickering observed in SECAM at sharp horizontal transients (due to the fact that one chrominance comes from the current line and the second comes from the preceding one), C_b and C_r samples are obtained by interpolating 4:2:2 samples of the two successive lines they will 'colourize' at display time.

This 4:2:0 format is of special importance as it is the input format used for D2-MAC and MPEG-2 (MP@ML) coding.

The SIF format (source intermediate format)

This format is obtained by halving the spatial resolution in both directions as well as the temporal resolution, which becomes 25 Hz for 625 line systems and 29.97 Hz for 525 line systems. Depending on the originating standard, the spatial resolutions are then:

- luminance resolution: 360 × 288 (625 lines) or 360 × 240 (525 lines)

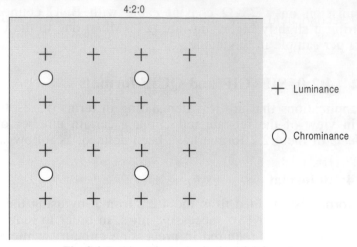

Fig. 2.4 Position of samples in the 4:2:0 format

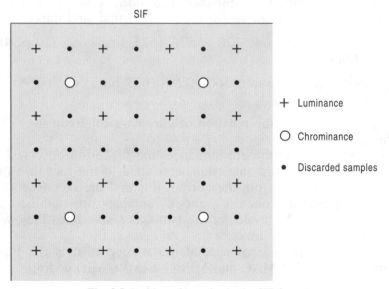

Fig. 2.5 Position of samples in the SIF format

- chrominance resolution: 180×144 (625 lines) or 180×120 (525 lines).

Figure 2.5 illustrates the position of the samples in the SIF format. Horizontal resolution is obtained by filtering and subsampling the input signal. The reduction in temporal and vertical resolution is normally obtained by interpolating samples of the odd and even fields, but is sometimes achieved by simply dropping every second field of the interlaced input format. The resolution obtained is the base for MPEG-1 encoding, and is giving a so-called 'VHS-like' quality in terms of resolution.

The CIF format (common intermediate format)

This is a compromise between European and American SIF formats: spatial resolution is taken from the 625 line SIF (360 × 288) and temporal resolution from the 525 line SIF (29.97 Hz). It is the basis used for video conferencing.

The QCIF format (quarter CIF)

Once again, this reduces the spatial resolution by 4 (2 in each direction) and the temporal resolution by 2 or 4 (15 or 7.5 Hz). It is the input format used for ISDN videotelephony using the H261 compression algorithm.

2.3 Transport problems

It is clear that a bit-rate of the order of 200 Mb/s, as required by the 4:2:2 format, cannot be used for direct broadcast to the end user, as it would occupy a bandwidth of the order of 40 MHz with a **64-QAM** modulation (6 bits/symbol) used for cable, or 135 MHz with a **QPSK** modulation (2 bits/symbol) used for satellite. This would represent 5–6 times the bandwidth required for transmission of an analogue PAL or SECAM signal, and does not even take into account any error correction algorithm (these concepts will be explained later in Chapters 6 and 7 on channel coding and modulation).

Compression algorithms, however, have been in use for some years for contribution links in the field of professional video, which reduce this bit-rate down to 34 Mb/s, but this is still too high for consumer applications, as it does not give any advantage in terms of capacity over existing analogue transmissions. It was the belief that this problem would not be solved economically in the foreseeable future (in large part due to the cost of the memory size required) that gave birth in the 1980s to hybrid standards such as D2-MAC (analogue video, digital sound) and delayed the introduction of 100% digital video. However, the very rapid progress made in compression techniques and IC technology in the second half of the 1980s made these systems obsolete soon after their introduction.

The essential conditions required to start digital television broadcast services were the development of technically and economically viable solutions to problems which can be classified into two main categories:

- *Source coding* – this is the technical term for compression. It encompasses all video and audio compression techniques used to reduce as much as possible the bit-rate (in terms of Mb/s required to transmit moving pictures of a given resolution and the associated sound) with the lowest perceptible degradation in quality.

- *Channel coding* – this consists of developing powerful error correction algorithms associated with the most spectrally efficient modulation techniques (in terms of Mb/s per MHz), taking into account the available bandwidth and the foreseeable imperfections of the transmission channel.

Taking into account the fact that many programmes can be transmitted on one RF channel, the sequence of operations to be performed on the transmitter side is roughly as illustrated in Fig. 2.6. We will follow the order of the functional boxes in this figure when we discuss them in the following chapters.

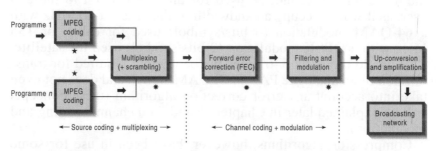

Fig. 2.6 Sequence of main operations on the broadcasting side

Note 2.1

The CCIR was the radiocommunication branch of the former CCITT (Comité Consultatif International du Télégraphe et du Téléphone), recently renamed the ITU (International Telecommunications Union). The CCIR is now called the ITU-R.

Note 2.2

For some multimedia applications (video in PCs mainly), other sampling frequencies are often used in order to obtain so-called **square pixels** to ease mixing of live video and computer images without aspect ratio distortion. In fact, the aspect ratio of a standard TV picture and of a computer display is 4/3 (ratio of the width to the height of the picture); in order to have identical resolutions in the horizontal and vertical directions, which is the case for today's computer display formats, it is necessary that the ratio of the number of pixels per line to the number of useful lines is 4/3. This is not the case for CCIR-601 derived formats, neither in 625 line standards (720/576 < 4/3) nor in 525 line standards (720/480 > 4/3).

For 525 line standards (480 useful lines), square pixels imply $480 \times 4/3 = 640$ pixels/line, which is obtained with a sampling frequency of 12.2727 MHz. This is not an accident since this resolution of 640×480 corresponds to the basic VGA graphics mode – this mode is, in fact, an *uninterlaced* or progressive variant of the NTSC scanning standard (line frequency = 31 468 Hz, frame frequency = 59.94 Hz). For 625 line standards (576 useful lines), square pixels imply $576 \times 4/3 = 768$ pixels/line, which requires a sampling frequency of 14.75 MHz.

Note 2.3

Dynamic

The dynamic D of a signal with a maximum peak-to-peak amplitude V_{PP}, quantized with m steps (with $m = 2^b$, where b is the number of bits of the quantization), is the ratio between V_{PP} and the maximum peak value of the quantization error, which is equal to the quantization step Q.

By definition, Q is equal to the maximum peak-to-peak amplitude V_{PP} divided by the number of quantization steps m, i.e. $Q = V_{PP}/m = V_{PP}/2^b$. Hence, the dynamic D (in dB) is equal to

$$D \text{ (dB)} = 20 \times \log (V_{PP}/Q) = 20 \times \log (V_{PP} \times 2^b/V_{PP})$$
$$= 20 \times \log 2^b = b \times 20 \times \log 2$$

Hence

$$D \cong b \times 6 \text{ dB}$$

Example 1 (video). A quantization with 8 bits (b = 8) results in D ≅ 48 dB.

Example 2 (audio). A quantization with 16 bits (b = 16) results in D ≅ 96 dB.

Signal to quantization noise ratio

If Q is the quantization step, the **quantization noise** voltage N_q is equal to $Q/\sqrt{12}$.

For a video signal, V_{PP} is equal to the black-to-white amplitude V_{BW}, and so $Q = V_{BW}/m = V_{BW}/2^b$. The signal to quantization noise ratio, S_V/N_q, is the ratio of the black-to-white signal V_{BW} to the quantization noise voltage N_q:

$$S_V/N_q \text{ (dB)} = 20 \times \log (V_{BW} \times 2^b \times \sqrt{12}/V_{BW})$$
$$= 20 \times \log (2^b \times \sqrt{12}) \cong b \times 6 + 20 \times \log \sqrt{12}$$

or

$$S_V/N_q \cong D + 10.8 \text{ dB}$$

Therefore, in the case of example 1 above (video signal quantized with 8 bits), $D \cong 48$ dB and $S_V/N_q \cong 58.8$ dB.

For an audio signal, the signal to quantization noise ratio, S_A/N_q, is the ratio of the root mean square (RMS) signal V_{RMS} to the quantization noise voltage N_q. If we assume a sinusoidal signal of maximum peak-to-peak amplitude V_{PP}, the corresponding maximum RMS voltage is $V_{RMS} = V_{PP}/2\sqrt{2}$. Thus

$$S_A/N_q \text{ (dB)} = 20 \times \log (V_{PP} \times 2^b \times \sqrt{12}/V_{PP} \times 2\sqrt{2})$$
$$= 20 \times \log (2^b \times \sqrt{12}/2\sqrt{2})$$

$$S_A/N_q \text{ (dB)} \cong b \times 6 + 20 (\log \sqrt{12} - \log 2\sqrt{2})$$
$$\cong D + 20 \times 0.09$$

or

$$S_A/N_q \cong D + 1.8 \text{ dB}$$

Thus, in the case of example 2 (audio signal quantized with 16 bits), $D \cong 96$dB and $S_A/N_q \cong 97.8$ dB.

3 Source coding: compression of video and audio signals

In the preceding chapter, we explained why compression was an absolute must in order to be able to broadcast TV pictures in a channel of acceptable width. A spectrum bandwidth comparable to conventional analogue broadcasts (6–8 MHz for cable or terrestrial broadcasts, 27–36 MHz for satellite) implies in practice maximum bit-rates of the order of 30–40 Mb/s, with the necessary error correction algorithms and modulation schemes, which are explained in Chapters 6 and 7.

We will now examine the principles and various steps of video and audio compression which allow these bit-rates (and in fact much less) to be achieved, and which are currently being used in the various video/audio compression standards. These compression methods use general data compression algorithms applicable to any kind of data, and exploit the spatial redundancy (correlation of neighbouring points within an image) and the specificities of visual perception (lack of sensitivity of the eye to fine details) for fixed pictures (JPEG), and the very high temporal redundancy between successive images in the case of moving pictures (MPEG). In the same way, audio compression methods exploit particularities of the human aural perception to reduce bit-rates by eliminating inaudible information (psycho-acoustic coding).

3.1   Some general data compression principles

3.1.1   Run length coding (RLC)

When an information source emits successive message elements which can deliver relatively long series of identical elements (which, as explained later in this chapter, is the case with the DCT after thresholding and quantization), it is advantageous to transmit the code of this element and the number of successive occurrences rather than to repeat the code of the element; this gives a variable compression factor (the longer the series, the bigger the compression factor). This type of coding which does not lose any information is defined as **reversible**. This method is commonly employed for file compression related to disk storage or transmission by computers (zip etc.); it is also the method used in fax machines.

3.1.2   Variable length coding (VLC) or entropy coding

This bit-rate reduction method is based on the fact that the probability of occurrence of an element generated by a source and coded on n bits is sometimes not the same (i.e. equiprobable) for all elements among the 2^n different possibilities. This means that, in order to reduce the bit-rate required to transmit the sequences generated by the source, it is advantageous to encode the most frequent elements with less than n bits and the less frequent elements with more bits, resulting in an average length that is less than a fixed length of n bits.

However, if this is to be done in real time, it implies a previous knowledge of the probability of occurrence of each possible element generated by the source. We have this knowledge, for example, in the case of the letters of the alphabet in a given language, and this allows this method to be used for text compression. This method is also valid for video images compressed by means of DCT, where energy is concentrated on a relatively small number of coefficients, as opposed to the temporal representation of the video signal where all values are almost equiprobable.

One can demonstrate that the information quantity Q transmitted by an element is equal to the logarithm (base 2) of the inverse of its probability of appearance p:

$$Q = \log_2 (1/p) = -\log_2 (p)$$

The sum of the information quantity of all elements generated by a source multiplied by their probability of appearance is called the entropy, H, of the source:

$$H = \sum_i p_i \log_2 (1/p_i)$$

The goal of variable length coding (VLC), or entropy coding, is to approach, as near as is possible, the entropic bit-rate (corresponding to an averaged number of bits per element as near as possible to the source's entropy). The most well-known method for variable length coding is the Huffmann algorithm, which assumes previous knowledge of the probability of each element. It works in the following way (illustrated in Fig. 3.1):

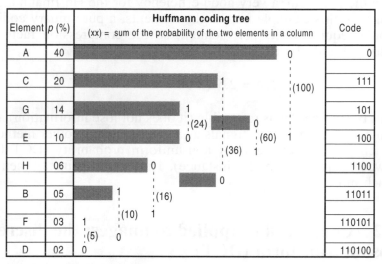

Fig. 3.1 Application of the Huffmann coding algorithm (grey zones indicate horizontal links)

- Each element is classified in order of decreasing probability, forming an 'occurrence table' (left part of Fig. 3.1).

- The two elements of lowest probability are then grouped into one element, the probability of which is the sum of the two probabilities. Bit '0' is attributed to the element of lowest probability and '1' to the other element; this reduces by one the number of elements to be classified.

- The new element is then grouped in the same way with the element having the next highest probability. '0' and '1' are attributed in the same way as above, and the process is continued until all the elements have been coded (sum of the probability of the last two elements = 100%).

- In this way, the Huffmann coding tree is built (central part of Fig. 3.1): the code for each element is obtained by positioning sequentially the bits encountered in moving along the Huffmann tree from left to right.

To illustrate this method, we have assumed a source generating eight elements with the following probabilities: $p(A) = 40\%$, $p(B) = 5\%$, $p(C) = 20\%$, $p(D) = 2\%$, $p(E) = 10\%$, $p(F) = 3\%$, $p(G) = 14\%$, $p(H) = 6\%$. In this example, the average word length after coding (sum of the products of the number of bits of each element and its probability) is 2.51 bits, while the entropy $H = \Sigma_i\, p_i \log_2 (1/p_i)$ is equal to 2.44 bits; this is only 3% more than the optimum, a very good efficiency for the Huffmann algorithm. In this example with eight elements, a pure binary coding would require 3 bits per element, so the compression factor η achieved with the Huffmann coding is

$$\eta = 2.51/3.00 = 83.7\%$$

This type of coding is reversible (it does not lose information) and can be applied to video signals as a complement to other methods which generate elements of non-uniform probability (DCT followed by quantization for instance). The overall gain can then be much more important.

3.2   Compression applied to images: the discrete cosine transform (DCT)

The discrete cosine transform is a particular case of the Fourier transform applied to discrete (sampled) signals, which decomposes a periodic signal into a series of sine and cosine harmonic functions. The signal can then be represented by a series of coefficients of each of these functions.

Without developing the mathematical details, we will simply indicate that, under certain conditions, the DCT decomposes the signal into only one series of harmonic cosine functions in phase with the signal, which reduces by half the number of coefficients necessary to describe the signal compared to a Fourier transform.

In the case of pictures, the original signal is a sampled bidimensional signal, and so we will also have a bidimensional DCT (horizontal and vertical directions), which will transform the luminance (or chrominance) discrete values of a block of $N \times N$ pixels into another block (or matrix) of $N \times N$ coefficients representing the amplitude of each of the cosine harmonic functions.

In the transformed block, coefficients on the horizontal axis represent increasing horizontal frequencies from left to right, and on the vertical axis they represent increasing vertical frequencies from top to bottom. The first coefficient in the top left corner (coordinates: 0, 0) represents null horizontal and vertical frequencies, and is therefore called the **DC** coefficient, and the bottom right coefficient represents the highest spatial frequency component in the two directions.

In order to reduce the complexity of the circuitry and the processing time required, the block size chosen is generally 8 × 8 pixels (Fig. 3.2), which the DCT transforms into a matrix of 8 × 8 coefficients (Fig. 3.3). A visual representation of the individual contribution of each coefficient to the appearance of the original block of 8 × 8 pixels can be seen in Fig. 3.4: the

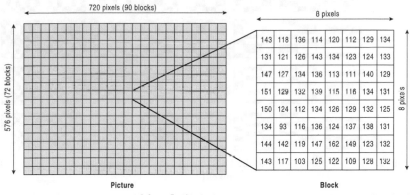

Fig. 3.2 Cutting out blocks of 8 × 8 pixels (values represent the luminance of a pixel)

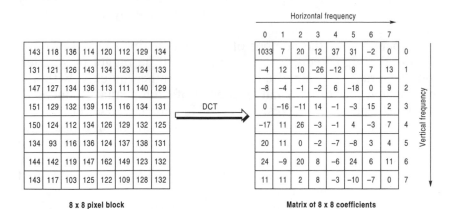

Fig. 3.3 Transformation of a block of 8 × 8 pixels into a matrix of 8 × 8 coefficients using the DCT

Horizontal frequency

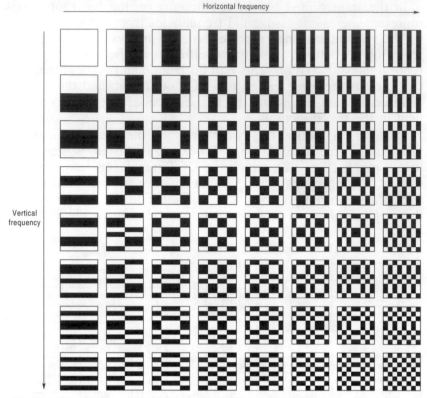

Vertical
frequency

Fig. 3.4 Contribution of each of the DCT coefficients to the appearance of the 8 × 8 pixel block

appearance of the original picture block can be obtained by averaging each of the 64 squares in Fig. 3.4 by its coefficient and summing the results.

Depending on the number of details contained in the original block, the high frequency coefficients will be bigger or smaller, but generally the amplitude decreases rather quickly with the frequency, due to the smaller energy of high spatial frequencies in most 'natural' images. The DCT thus has the remarkable property of concentrating the energy of the block on a relatively low number of coefficients situated in the top left corner of the matrix. In addition, these coefficients are decorrelated from each other. These two properties will be used to advantage in the next steps of the compression process.

Up to this point, there is no information loss: the DCT transform process is reversible. However, due to the psycho-physiological specificities of human vision (reduced sensitivity to high spatial frequencies), it is possible, without perceptible degradation of the picture quality, to eliminate the values below a certain threshold function of the frequency. The eliminated values are replaced by 0 (an operation known as **thresholding**); this part of the process is obviously not reversible, as some data are thrown away. The remaining coefficients are then quantized with an accuracy decreasing with the increasing spatial frequencies, which once again reduces the quantity of information required to encode a block; here again the process is not reversible, but it has little effect on the perceived picture quality. The thresholding/quantization process is illustrated in Fig. 3.5.

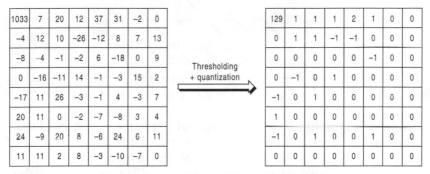

Fig. 3.5 Result of thresholding and quantization

The thresholding and quantization parameters can be used dynamically to regulate the bit-rate required to transmit moving pictures, as will be explained in Section 3.4.

A serial bitstream is obtained by 'zig-zag' reading of the coefficients, as shown in Fig. 3.6. This method is one of those allowing a relatively long series of null coefficients to be obtained as quickly as possible, in order to increase the efficiency of the following steps – run length coding followed by variable length coding (see Section 3.1).

3.3   Compression of fixed pictures

The first applications aimed at reducing the amount of information required for coding fixed pictures appeared in the 1980s, and they had as their primary objective the significant reduction of the size of graphics files and photographs in view of storing or transmitting them. In 1990, the **ISO** (International Standard Organization) created an international working group called JPEG

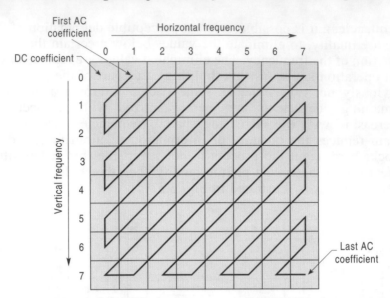

Fig. 3.6 'Zig-zag' reading of the coefficients of the matrix

(Joint Photographic Experts Group) which had the task of elaborating an international compression standard for fixed pictures of various resolutions in $Y\,C_r\,C_b$ or RGB format. The resulting international standard (widely known as JPEG) was published in 1993 under the reference ISO/IEC 10918, and it can be considered as a toolbox for fixed picture compression. We will not describe it in detail, as it is not the object of this book, but we will nevertheless go through its main steps, as it has largely inspired the way in which MPEG works.

It should be noted that JPEG compression can be either **lossy** or **lossless** (reversible), depending on the application and the desired compression factor. Most common applications use the lossy method, which allows compression factors of more than 10 to be achieved without noticeable picture quality degradation, depending on the picture content. We will only examine the case of lossy JPEG compression, as the coding of **I** (intra) pictures of MPEG uses the same process; lossless JPEG compression uses a different predictive coding which is not based on DCT, so we will not discuss it here.

Lossy JPEG compression can be described in six main steps:

1. *Decomposition of the picture into blocks* – the picture, generally in $Y\,C_b\,C_r$ format, is divided into elementary blocks of 8×8 pixels (Fig. 3.2), which represents for a 4:2:2 CCIR-601 picture a total number of 6480 luminance (Y) blocks and 3240 blocks for each C_r and C_b component. Each block is made up

of 64 numbers ranging from 0 to 255 (when digitized on 8 bits) for luminance, and -128 to $+127$ for chrominance C_r and C_b.

2. *Discrete cosine transform* – as explained previously, the DCT applied to each $Y\ C_b\ C_r$ block generates for each one a new 8×8 matrix made up of the coefficients of increasing spatial frequency as one moves away from the origin (upper left corner) which contains the DC component representing the average luminance or chrominance of the block. The value of these coefficients decreases quickly when going away from the origin of the matrix, and the final values are generally a series of small numbers or even zeroes. So, if the block is of uniform luminance or chrominance, only the DC coefficient will not be zero, and only this coefficient will have to be transmitted.

3. *Thresholding and quantization* – this step takes into account the specificities of human vision, particularly the fact that the eye does not distinguish fine details below a certain luminance level. It consists of zeroing the coefficients below a predetermined threshold, and quantizing the remaining ones with decreasing accuracy as the frequency increases. Contrary to the 63 other (AC) coefficients, the DC coefficient is **DPCM** coded (differential pulse code modulation) relative to the DC coefficient of the previous block, which allows a more accurate coding with a given number of bits. This allows the visibility of the blocks on the reconstructed picture to be reduced, as the eye, although not very sensitive to fine details, is nevertheless very sensitive to small luminance differences on uniform zones.

4. *Zig-zag scan* – except for the DC coefficient, which is treated separately, the 63 AC coefficients are read using a zig-zag scan (Fig. 3.6) in order to transform the matrix into a flow of data best suited for the next coding steps (RLC/VLC).

5. *Run length coding* – in order to make the best possible use of the long series of zeroes produced by the quantization and the zig-zag scan, the number of occurrences of zero is coded, followed by the next non-zero value, which reduces the amount of information to transmit.

6. *Variable length coding (Huffmann coding)* – this last step uses a conversion table in order to encode the most frequently occurring values with a short length, and the less frequent values

with a longer one. These last two steps (RLC and VLC) alone ensure a compression factor of between 2 and 3.

When the compression/decompression time is not of prime importance, which is often the case for fixed pictures, all the above-described steps can be done entirely using software. There are, however, a number of specialized processors which can speed up this process very much. The simplified principle of a JPEG decoder can be seen in the block diagram in Fig. 3.7.

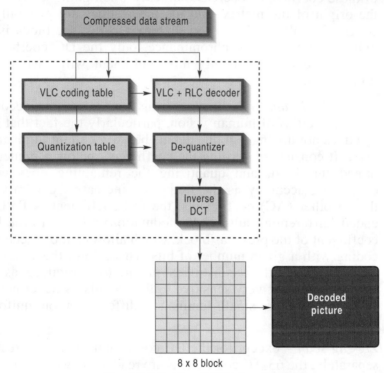

Fig. 3.7 Principle of JPEG decoding

3.4   Compression of moving pictures (MPEG)

In 1990, the need to store and reproduce moving pictures and the associated sound in digital format for multimedia applications on various platforms led the ISO to form an expert group along the same lines as JPEG, with members coming from the numerous branches involved (computer industry, telecoms, consumer electronics, semiconductors, broadcasters, universities, etc.); this group was called MPEG (Motion Pictures Experts Group).

The first outcome of its work was the International Standard ISO/IEC 11172, widely known as MPEG-1. The main goal was to allow the storage on CD-ROM or CD-I (single speed at that time) of live video and stereo sound, which implied a maximum bit-rate of 1.5 Mb/s. In addition to the intrinsic spatial redundancy exploited by JPEG for fixed pictures, coding of moving pictures allows exploitation of the very important temporal redundancy between successive pictures which make up a video sequence.

Given the very high compression rate objective for these applications (more than 100 compared to the original 4:2:2/CCIR 601 picture), the difficulty of the task is reduced from the beginning of the process by sacrificing the resolution. The format chosen for the pictures to be encoded is the SIF format (described in Section 2.2.2 – uninterlaced pictures, 360 × 288 @ 25 Hz or 360 × 240 @ 30 Hz depending on the original video standard), which corresponds roughly to the resolution of a consumer video recorder.

The sound compression algorithm used for the accompanying audio channels is known as **MUSICAM**, also used in the European digital radio system (**DAB**, Digital Audio Broadcasting). We will examine the principles of audio compression in Section 3.5.

The MPEG-1 standard consists of three distinct parts, published in November 1992:

- MPEG-1 system (ISO/IEC 11172-1): defines the MPEG-1 multiplex structure (cf. Chapter 4)

- MPEG-1 video (ISO/IEC 11172-2): defines MPEG-1 video coding

- MPEG-1 audio (ISO/IEC 11172-3): defines MPEG-1 audio coding.

However, the picture quality of MPEG-1 was not suitable for broadcast applications, since, among other things, it did not take into account the coding of interlaced pictures or evolution towards HDTV. The MPEG group thus worked on the definition of a flexible standard optimized for broadcasting. This international standard is known as MPEG-2.

As its predecessor, MPEG-2 is specified in three distinct parts, published in November 1994:

- MPEG-2 system (ISO/IEC 13818-1): defines the MPEG-2 streams (cf. Chapter 4)

- MPEG-2 video (ISO/IEC 13818-2): defines MPEG-2 video coding

- MPEG-2 audio (ISO/IEC 13818-3): defines MPEG-2 audio coding.

MPEG-2 is, among other things, the source coding standard used by the European DVB (Digital Video Broadcasting) TV broadcasting system, which is the result of the work started in 1991 by the ELG (European Launching Group), later to become the DVB committee.

3.4.1　Principles behind the video coding of MPEG-1 (multimedia applications)

As indicated previously, the main objective for MPEG-1 was to reach a medium quality video with a constant total bit-rate of 1.5 Mb/s for storing video and audio on CD-ROM. The video part uses 1.15 Mb/s, the remaining 350 kb/s being used by audio and additional data required by the system and other information. However, the MPEG-1 specification is very flexible and allows different parameters to be chosen depending on the compromise between encoder complexity, compression rate and quality.

The video coding uses the same principles as lossy JPEG, to which new techniques are added to form the MPEG-1 'toolbox'; these techniques exploit the strong correlation between successive pictures in order to considerably reduce the amount of information required to transmit or store them. These techniques, known as 'prediction with movement compensation', consist of deducing most of the pictures of a sequence from preceding and even subsequent pictures, with a minimum of additional information representing the differences between pictures. This requires the presence in the MPEG encoder of a **movement estimator**, which is the most complex function and greatly determines the encoder's performance; fortunately, this function is not required in the decoder.

As we are talking about moving pictures, decoding has to be accomplished in real time (this means an acceptable and constant processing delay); this implies, for the time being at least, some specialized hardware. The coding, which is much more complex, can be done in more than one 'pass' for applications where real time is not required but where quality is of prime importance (engraving of disks for instance); real time (which does not mean null processing time) will, however, be required for many applications, such as 'live' video transmissions.

The practical realization of the encoder is therefore a trade-off between speed, compression rate, complexity and picture quality. In addition, synchronization time and random access time to a sequence have to be maintained within an acceptable limit (not exceeding 0.5 s), which restricts the maximum number of pictures that can be dependent on the first picture to between 10 and 12 for a system operating at 25 pictures/s.

The different types of MPEG pictures

MPEG defines three types of pictures (Note 3.1) which are arranged as shown in Fig. 3.8.

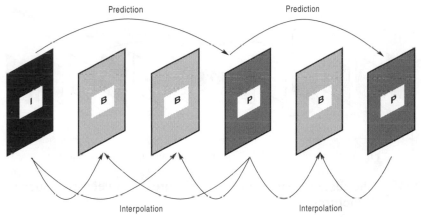

Fig. 3.8 Concatenation of the three types of pictures in MPEG

- **I (intra) pictures** are coded without reference to other pictures, in a very similar manner to JPEG, which means that they contain all the information necessary for their reconstruction by the decoder; for this reason, they are the essential entry point for access to a video sequence. The compression rate of I pictures is relatively low, and is comparable to a JPEG coded picture of a similar resolution.

- **P (predicted) pictures** are coded from the preceding I or P picture, using the techniques of motion compensated prediction. P pictures can be used as the basis for next predicted pictures, but since motion compensation is not perfect, it is not possible to extend very much the number of P pictures between two I pictures. The compression rate of P pictures is significantly higher than for I pictures.

- **B (bidirectional or bidirectionally predicted) pictures** are coded by bidirectional interpolation between the I or P picture which precedes and follows them. As they are not used for coding subsequent pictures, B pictures do not propagate coding errors. B pictures offer the highest compression rate.

Depending on the complexity of the encoder used, it is possible to encode I only, I and P, or I, P and B pictures, with very different results with regard to compression rate and random access resolution, and also with regard to encoding time and perceived quality.

Two parameters, M and N, describe the succession of I, P and B pictures (Fig. 3.9):

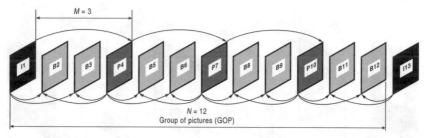

Fig. 3.9 Example of an MPEG group of pictures for $N = 3$ and $M = 12$

- M is the distance (in number of pictures) between two successive P pictures;

- N is the distance between two successive I pictures, defining a 'group of pictures' (**GOP**).

The parameters generally used are $M = 3$ and $N = 12$, in order to obtain a satisfactory video quality with an acceptable random access time (< 0.5 s) within a bit-rate of 1.15 Mb/s. With these parameters, a video sequence is made up as follows: 1/12 of its pictures are I pictures (8.33%), 1/4 are P pictures (25%) and 2/3 are B pictures (66%); the global compression rate is maximized by the fact that the most frequent pictures have the highest compression rate.

Re-ordering of the pictures

It is obvious that the sequence of the pictures after decoding has to be in the same order as the original sequence before encoding.

With the above parameters ($M = 3$, $N = 12$), the correspondence between the original picture number and its coded type is as follows:

1(I) 2(B) 3(B) 4(P) 5(B) 6(B) 7(P) 8(B) 9(B) 10(P) 11(B) 12(B)
13(I) . . .

However, in order to encode or decode a B (bidirectional) picture, both the encoder and the decoder will need the I or P preceding picture and the I or P subsequent picture. This requires re-ordering of the original picture sequence such that the decoder and the encoder have at their disposal the required I and/or P pictures before the B pictures are processed. The re-ordering thus gives the following sequence:

1(I) 4(P) 2(B) 3(B) 7(P) 5(B) 6(B) 10(P) 8(B) 9(B) 13(I) 11(B)
12(B) . . .

The increase in compression rate permitted by the B pictures has to be paid for by an increase in encoding delay (two extra picture durations) and in the memory size required for both encoding and decoding (one extra picture to store).

Decomposition of an MPEG video sequence in layers

MPEG defines a hierarchy of **layers** within a video sequence, as illustrated in Fig. 3.10. Each of these layers has specific function(s) in the MPEG process. Starting from the top level, the successive layers are:

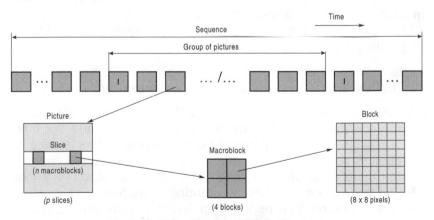

Fig. 3.10 Hierarchy of the MPEG video layers

- **Sequence** – this is the highest layer which defines the context valid for the whole sequence (basic video parameters, etc.).

- **Group of pictures (GOP)** – this is the layer determining the random access to the sequence, which always starts with an I picture. In the above example ($M = 3$, $N = 12$), the GOP is made up of 12 pictures.

- **Picture** – this is the elementary display unit, which can be of one of the three types (I, P or B).

- **Slice** – this is the layer for intra frame addressing and (re)synchronization, for instance for error recovery. It is defined as a suite of contiguous macroblocks. The ensemble of the slices covers the whole picture without any overlap between different slices. The size of a slice can theoretically range from one macroblock to the whole picture, but it is often a complete row of macroblocks.

- **Macroblock** – this is the layer used for movement estimation/compensation. A macroblock has a size of 16×16 pixels and is made up of four blocks of luminance and two blocks of chrominance (one C_r and one C_b) covering the same area (Fig. 3.11).

- **Block** – as in JPEG, a picture is divided in blocks of 8×8 pixels. The block is the layer where the DCT takes place.

Owing to the division of the picture into an integer number of macroblocks, the horizontal resolution of MPEG-1/SIF is reduced to 352 pixels for luminance (22 macroblocks) from the 360 pixels of the original SIF picture, since 360 is not a multiple of 16. The effective resolution is then 352×288 @ 25 Hz ($22 \times 18 = 396$ macroblocks) for pictures originating from 625 line systems, and 352×240 @ 30 Hz ($22 \times 15 = 330$ macroblocks) for pictures originating from 525 line systems.

Prediction, motion estimation and compensation

We have indicated before that P and B pictures were 'predicted' from preceding and/or subsequent pictures. We will now see how.

In a sequence of moving pictures, moving objects lead to differences between corresponding zones of consecutive pictures, so that there is no obvious correlation between these two zones. *Motion estimation* consists of defining a *motion vector* which ensures the correlation between an 'arrival' zone on the second picture and a 'departure' zone on the first picture, using a

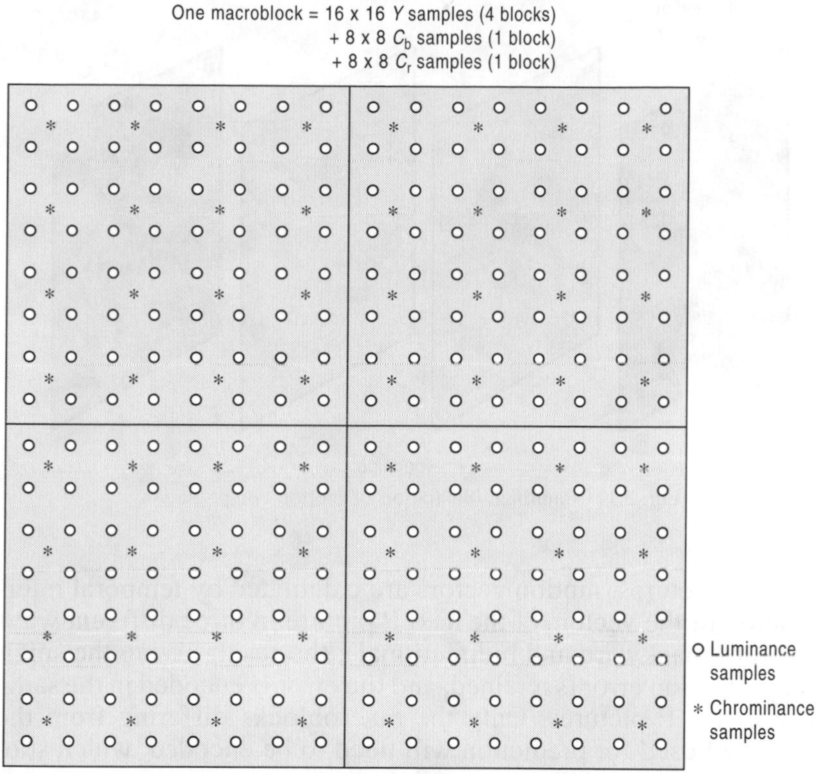

One macroblock = 16 x 16 *Y* samples (4 blocks)
+ 8 x 8 C_b samples (1 block)
+ 8 x 8 C_r samples (1 block)

o Luminance
samples

* Chrominance
samples

Fig. 3.11 Composition of a 4:2:0 macroblock (o = *Y* samples,* = C_b and C_r samples)

technique known as *block matching*. This is done at the macroblock level (16 × 16 pixels) by moving a macroblock of the current picture within a small search window from the previous picture, and comparing it to all possible macroblocks of the window in order to find the one that is most similar. The difference in position of the two matching macroblocks gives a motion vector (Fig. 3.12) which will be applied to all three components of the macroblock (Y, C_b, C_r).

In comparing a P picture and an I picture, or two P pictures, due to the temporal distance between these pictures (three pictures in the case of $M = 3$, $N = 12$), block matching will generally not be perfect and motion vectors can be of relatively high amplitude. That is why the difference (or *prediction error*) between the actual block to be encoded and the matching block is calculated, and encoded in a similar way to the blocks of the I pictures (DCT, quantization, RLC/VLC). This process is called *motion compensation*.

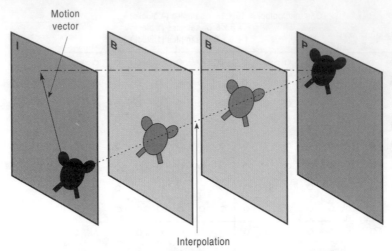

Fig. 3.12 Simplified illustration of motion compensation

For B pictures, motion vectors are calculated by temporal inter-polation of the vectors of the next P picture in three different ways (forward, backward and bidirectional); the result giving the smal-lest prediction error is retained, and the error is encoded in the same way as for P pictures. Only the macroblocks differing from the picture(s) used for prediction will need to be encoded, which sub-stantially reduces the amount of information required for coding B and P pictures. As the size of the moving objects is generally bigger than a macroblock, there is a strong correlation between the motion vectors of consecutive blocks, and a differential coding method (DPCM) is used to encode the vectors, thus reducing the number of bits required. When the 'prediction' does not give a usable result (for instance in the case of a moving camera where completely new zones appear in the picture), the corresponding parts of the picture are 'intra' coded, in the same way as for I pictures.

Output bit-rate control

The bitstream generated by the video (or audio) encoder is called the *elementary stream* (**ES**). In order to fulfil the constraints of the channel (transmission or recording/playback) and of the spe-cified input buffer for the reference MPEG decoder, the bit-rate of this elementary stream must generally be kept constant. This is not guaranteed by the coding process described above, taking into account the very differing amounts of detail and movement in the pictures to be encoded.

In order to control the bit-rate at the output of the encoder, the encoder output is equipped with a **FIFO** buffer; the amount of information held in this buffer is monitored and maintained within predetermined limits by means of a feedback loop modifying the quantization parameters, which have a major influence on the bit-rate of the encoded bitstream. In this way, it is possible to obtain a constant bit-rate, with a resolution that depends on the picture content and amount of movement in the picture (the more movement, the lower the resolution). A very schematic block diagram of an MPEG encoder, which gives only a poor idea of its real complexity, is shown in Fig. 3.13.

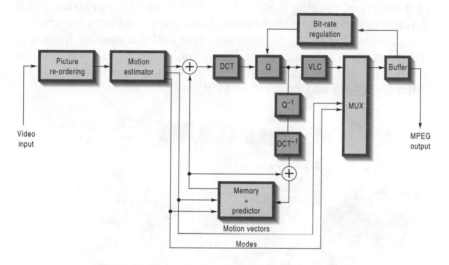

Fig. 3.13 Schematic diagram of the MPEG encoder

The decoder (Fig. 3.14) does not have to perform motion estimation and so is much simpler, which was one of the main objectives of the standard, as there will be many more decoders than encoders, the application of MPEG being mostly 'asymmetric'.

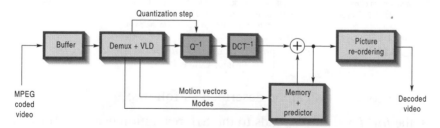

Fig. 3.14 Schematic diagram of the MPEG decoder

3.4.2   Video coding of MPEG-2 (broadcast applications)

MPEG-2 can be described as a 'compression toolbox'. It is more complex than MPEG-1, to which it can be considered a superset, since it uses all the MPEG-1 tools and adds some new ones. MPEG-2 is also upwards compatible with MPEG-1, which means that an MPEG-2 decoder can decode all MPEG-1 compliant elementary streams.

MPEG-2 levels and profiles

The MPEG-2 standard has four **levels** which define the resolution of the picture, ranging from SIF to HDTV, and five **profiles** which determine the set of compression tools used, and hence there is a compromise between compression rate and the cost of the decoder. Certain combinations of levels and profiles of little interest are not used. Fig. 3.15 illustrates the main characteristics of the different levels and profiles of MPEG-2.

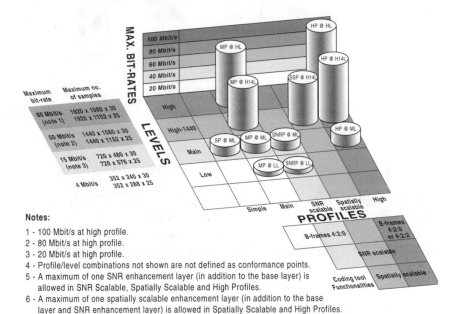

Notes:

1 - 100 Mbit/s at high profile.
2 - 80 Mbit/s at high profile.
3 - 20 Mbit/s at high profile.
4 - Profile/level combinations not shown are not defined as conformance points.
5 - A maximum of one SNR enhancement layer (in addition to the base layer) is allowed in SNR Scalable, Spatially Scalable and High Profiles.
6 - A maximum of one spatially scalable enhancement layer (in addition to the base layer and SNR enhancement layer) is allowed in Spatially Scalable and High Profiles.

Fig. 3.15 MPEG-2 levels and profiles (source: *Going ahead with Digital Television*; © DVB Project Office 1995)

The four levels can be described as follows:

- the *low level* corresponds to the SIF resolution used in MPEG-1 (up to 360 × 288);

- the *main level* corresponds to standard 4:2:0 resolution (up to 720 × 576);

- the *high-1440 level* is aimed at HDTV (resolution up to 1440 × 1152);

- the *high level* is optimized for wide screen HDTV (resolution up to 1920 × 1152).

In the case of profiles, it is a little more complicated:

- The *simple profile* is defined in order to simplify the encoder and the decoder, at the expense of a higher bit-rate, as it does not use bidirectional prediction (B pictures).

- The *main profile* is today the best compromise between compression rate and cost, as it uses all three image types (I, P, B) but leads to a more complex encoder and decoder.

- The *scalable profiles* (hierarchy coding) are intended for future use. They will allow transmission of a basic quality picture (*base layer*) in terms of spatial resolution (spatially scalable profile) or quantization accuracy (SNR scalable profile), and of supplementary information (*enhanced layer*) allowing the picture characteristics to be enhanced. This could be used, for instance, to transmit in a compatible way the same programme in basic resolution on standard decoders and in higher resolution on special HD decoders, or alternatively to allow a basic quality reception in the case of difficult receiving conditions and enhanced quality in good receiving conditions (terrestrial TV).

- The *high profile* is intended for HDTV broadcast applications in 4:2:0 or 4:2:2 format.

There is an ascending compatibility between profiles, and a decoder of a given profile will be able to decode all lower profiles (left part of Fig. 3.15).

The most important combination in the short term, as it is the one retained for consumer broadcast applications in Europe, is known as *main profile at main level* (MP@ML). It corresponds to MPEG-2 encoding of interlaced pictures in 4:2:0 format with a resolution of 720 × 480 @ 30 Hz or 720 × 576 @ 25 Hz, with a toolbox including coding of I, P and B pictures. Depending on the compromise struck between bit-rate and picture quality and the nature of the pictures to be transmitted, the bit-rate will generally be between 4 Mb/s (giving a quality similar to PAL or SECAM) and 9 Mb/s (near CCIR-601 studio quality).

Apart from the resolution of the original picture and the processing of interlaced pictures, which we will discuss later, the complete process described in Section 3.4.1 for MPEG-1 is valid for MPEG-2 (MP@ML) encoding and decoding, and in particular the layer hierarchy (from block to sequence) shown in Fig. 3.10. There is a small difference, however, in the definition of the slices, as they do not necessarily cover the whole picture and are only made up of contiguous blocks of the same horizontal row (Fig. 3.16).

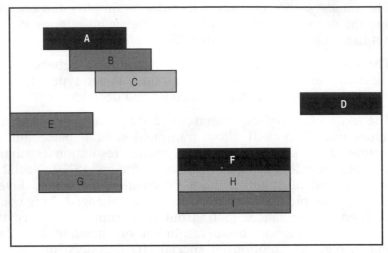

Fig. 3.16 The MPEG-2 slices in the most general case

If we exclude the levels and profiles, the main new feature of MPEG-2 compared to MPEG-1 is the processing of interlaced pictures, which introduces some complexity and certain specific modes. For best results, interlaced pictures will have to be processed in different ways depending on the importance of movements between the two fields of a picture: the extreme cases are, on the one hand, pictures originating from cinema films, where the two fields come from the same cinema picture (at least in 50 Hz systems), and on the other, TV pictures from sporting events where differences due to motion between the two fields of a picture can be important.

MPEG-2 specific prediction modes (interlaced pictures)

The temporal sequence of the vertical position of the lines belonging to successive fields in an interlaced system is shown in Fig. 3.17.

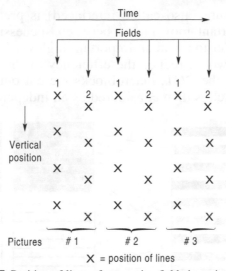

Fig. 3.17 Position of lines of successive fields in an interlaced system

For the intra coding of interlaced pictures, MPEG-2 permits one to choose between two image structures, a *frame* and a *field*:

- The frame structure (also called progressive) is best suited for cases where there is little movement between two successive fields. Macroblocks and blocks are then cut out of the complete frame (Fig. 3.18), and so the DCT is applied to consecutive vertical points separated from each other by a period of 20 ms (duration of a field in 50 Hz systems), which is no problem for the parts of the picture with little movement. In this mode, however, it is possible to code the most animated blocks in the inter-field mode, which means positioning the blocks in one field only.

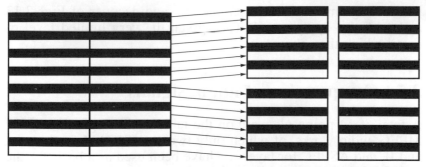

Fig. 3.18 Cutting blocks out of macroblocks (frame mode)

- The field structure (also called interlaced) is preferable when there are important movements between successive fields; in this case, in order to avoid an important high vertical frequency content which would reduce the efficiency of the compression steps following the DCT, macroblocks are cut out of one field (Fig. 3.19), which is then considered as an independent picture.

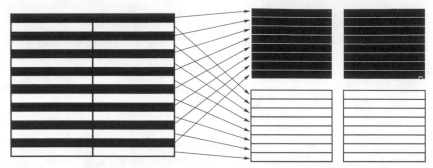

Fig. 3.19 Cutting blocks out of macroblocks (field mode)

In the case of motion estimation, different modes are also possible; a macroblock can be predicted in frame, field or mixed modes:

- In the frame mode, a macroblock taken from an odd field is used to predict a corresponding macroblock in the next odd field, and the same holds for even fields. The motion vectors correspond in this case to the duration of two fields (40 ms).

- In the field mode, the prediction of a macroblock is made using the preceding field, and motion vectors correspond to the duration of one field (20 ms).

- In the mixed mode, prediction is made from macroblocks belonging to two frames.

The diagrams of the MPEG encoder and decoder of Figs 3.13 and 3.14 also apply to MPEG-2, given the very limited level of detail which they show.

3.5   Compression of audio signals

A total of 14 proposals were on the table at the beginning of the MPEG audio works, of which only two (MUSICAM for layers I and II, and ASPEC for layer III) have been used as a basis for the final MPEG audio specification.

3.5.1   Principles of MPEG audio

Here again, the limitations of the human ear will be exploited in order to reduce the amount of information required to encode audio signals without deteriorating in a perceptible way the quality of the sound to be reproduced.

For a long time, it has been known that the human ear has a maximum sensitivity for audio frequencies ranging from 1 to 5 kHz. The sensitivity curve, which represents the audibility or perception threshold as a function of frequency in the absence of any 'disturbing' signal, is shown in Fig. 3.20, where it can be seen that signal A is audible, since it exceeds the audibility threshold.

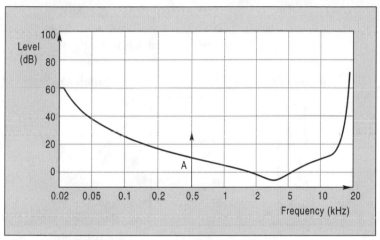

Fig. 3.20 Sensitivity of the ear as a function of frequency (signal A is audible)

More recently, however, it has been suggested that this curve is modified in the presence of multiple signals; for instance, in the case of two signals of relatively near frequencies, the strongest signal has the effect of increasing the perception threshold in the vicinity of its frequency, which makes the ear less sensitive in this frequency region. This effect is illustrated in Fig. 3.21, where it can be seen that signal A, previously audible, is now 'masked' by signal B which is more powerful than A. This effect is known as *frequency masking*.

There is also another effect called *temporal masking*: a sound of strong amplitude also masks sounds immediately preceding it or following it in time, as illustrated in Fig. 3.22.

In order to quantify these effects as precisely as possible, a lot of experiments have been conducted which have led to the definition

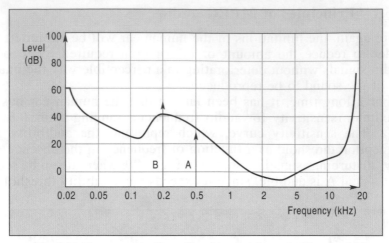

Fig. 3.21 Frequency masking effect (signal A is masked by signal B)

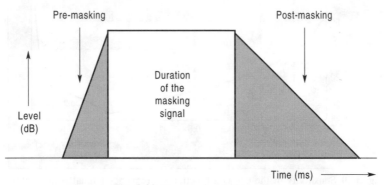

Fig. 3.22 Temporal masking effect

of a **psycho-acoustical model** of human hearing. This model was used as the basis for the conception of a *perceptual encoder*, characterized by a masking curve and a quantization of signals that vary as a function of the signals to be encoded.

The principle of the coding process consists of first dividing the audio frequency band into 32 sub-bands of equal width by means of a *polyphase* filter bank. The output signal from a sub-band filter corresponding to a duration of 32 **PCM** samples is called a **sub-band sample**. The principle of perceptual coding is illustrated in Fig. 3.23.

The psycho-acoustical model allows elimination of all sub-band signals below their perception threshold, as they would not be heard by the listener, and defines the required quantization accuracy for each sub-band in order that the quantization noise stays

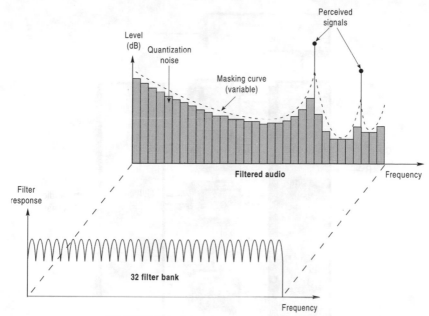

Fig. 3.23 Principle of perceptual audio coding

below the audibility threshold for this sub-band. In this way, frequency regions where the ear is more sensitive can be quantified with more accuracy than other regions. Simplified diagrams of the MPEG audio encoder and decoder are shown in Figs 3.24 and 3.25, respectively.

Analysis of the signal to determine the masking curve and quantization accuracy is not carried out for each PCM sample, being carried out instead in a time interval called a frame, which corresponds to the duration of 12×32 PCM samples (MPEG-1 layer 1) or 12×96 PCM samples (MPEG-1 layer 2). In this interval, the encoder has to evaluate the maximum amplitude of the signal in order to define a **scaling factor**, which is coded on 6 bits, covering a dynamic range of 128 dB in 64 steps of 2 dB. All information necessary for sound decoding is supplied at the frame level, which is the smallest unit for random access to the sequence (comparable to the group of pictures for video).

3.5.2   The MPEG audio layers

The MPEG audio standard defines three coding **layers** which offer very different compression rates for a given perceived audio quality.

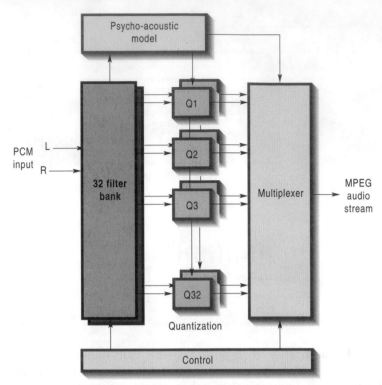

Fig. 3.24 Principle behind the MPEG audio encoder

- **Layer I** or 'pre-MUSICAM' – this uses the PASC algorithm (precision adaptive sub-band coding) developed by Philips for its DCC digital audio cassette. It uses one fixed bit-rate chosen among 14 possibles ranging from 32 to 448 kb/s; subjective hi-fi quality requires 192 kb/s per audio channel, and therefore 384 kb/s in stereo. The main advantage of layer I is the relative simplicity of the encoder and decoder.

  The psycho-acoustical model used is known as *model 1*. Quantization accuracy of the sub-band coefficients is defined for the whole duration of the frame by a 4 bit number which allows a coding from 0 to 15 bits for each sub-band, and the 6 bit scaling factor is also defined for the whole frame.

- **Layer II** – this is the main mode used in the DVB system and uses the algorithm known as MUSICAM which was developed for the European digital radio (DAB, digital audio broadcasting). For an equivalent audio quality, layer II requires a 30–50% smaller bit-rate than layer I, at the expense of a moderate increase in complexity for the encoder and the decoder. The bit-rate is fixed

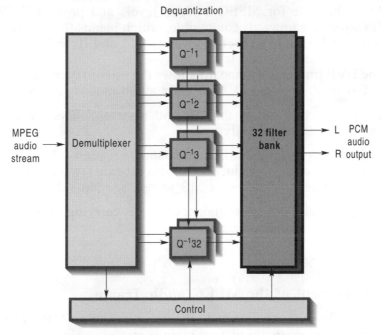

Fig. 3.25 Principle behind the MPEG audio decoder

and chosen from 32 to 192 kb/s per channel, the hi-fi quality being obtained from 128 kb/s per channel (256 kb/s in stereo).

The psycho-acoustical model used is the same as for layer I (model 1), but the frame duration is three times longer. In order to reduce the bit-rate, the quantization accuracy of the sub-band coefficients decreases with the frequency (quantization defined on 4 bits for low bands, 3 bits for medium bands and 2 bits for high bands) instead of the fixed format used in layer I. In addition, two or three consecutive sub-band samples can be grouped and coded with the same coefficient.

- **Layer III** – this is a recent development using a different psycho-acoustical model (model 2), a Huffmann coding and a DCT based signal analysis instead of the sub-band coding used in layers I and II. For a given quality, the compression rate achievable with layer III is approximately twice as high as with layer II, but the encoder and decoder are substantially more complex and the encoding/decoding time is much longer. Hi-fi quality requires only 64 kb/s per channel (128 kb/s for stereo).

Layer III is mainly intended for unidirectional applications on low bit-rate media (ISDN for instance), and its use is not foreseen for consumer digital TV broadcating, so we will not discuss it further.

As is the case for MPEG-2 video levels and profiles, MPEG audio layers are upwards compatible, which means that a layer III decoder will be able to decode also layers I and II, and a layer II decoder will also decode layer I.

The DVB digital TV standard allows the use of layers I and II of MPEG-1 audio (Note 3.2). Four main audio modes are possible:

- stereo – in this mode, the left and right channels are coded completely independently;

- **joint_stereo** – exploits the redundancy between left and right channels in order to reduce the audio bit-rate (two codings are possible: intensity_stereo or MS_stereo, see Note 3.3);

- dual_channel – two independent channels carrying uncorrelated sounds (e.g. bilingual);

- mono – only one audio channel.

3.5.3   Format of the MPEG audio frame

The audio frame is the elementary access unit to an MPEG audio sequence. It is made up of four main parts:

- a header of 32 bits
- parity (CRC) over 16 bits
- audio data of variable length
- ancillary data (AD) of variable length.

Format of the layer I frame (see Fig. 3.26)

The MPEG audio layer I frame represents 384 PCM samples of the audio signal, and contains 12 successive sub-band samples. As the number of samples is independent of the sampling frequency,

Header	CRC	AUDIO data				AD
System 32 bits	Parity 16 bits	Allocation bits/SBS	Scaling factors	Sub-band samples (SBS) (12 × 32 sub-band samples)		Ancillary data

- The header carries the synchronization and system information (see Table 3.1).
- The use of the parity (CRC) is optional.
- The 'bit allocation per SBS' field contains 32 integers coded on 4 bits, each of them defining the resolution for coding the samples of one of the 32 sub-bands.
- The 'scaling factors' field contains 32 integers coded on 6 bits, each of them giving the multiplication factor of the samples of one sub-band.

Fig. 3.26 Simplified representation of the MPEG audio layer I frame

Table 3.1 The fields of the MPEG audio frame header (all layers)

Field	Comment	No. of bits
Syncword	1111 1111 1111 (FFF hex)	12
ID	Always '1' for MPEG-1 audio	1
Layer	11 = I, 10 = II, 01 = III, 00 = reserved	2
Protection_bit	0 if redundancy is added, 1 otherwise	1
Bit-rate_index	15 values (0000 = user defined, 1111 = forbidden)	4
Sampling_frequency	00 = 44.1 kHz, 01 = 48, 10 = 32, 11 = reserved	2
Padding_bit	1 = padding (necessary at F_s = 44.1 kHz)	1
Private-bit	Not specified	1
Mode	00 = stereo, 01 = joint, 10 = dual, 11 = mono	2
Mode_extension	Sub-band range in intensity_stereo mode	2
Copyright	1 = copyright, 0 = free	1
Original/copy	1 = original, 0 = copy	1
Emphasis	00 = none, 01 = 50/75 μs, 10 = reserved, 11 = J17	2

the frame duration is inversely proportional to the sampling frequency. This duration is 12 ms at 32 kHz, 8.7 ms at 44.1 kHz and 8 ms at 48 kHz.

Format of the layer II frame (see Fig. 3.27)

In this case, the frame is made up of 12 **granules**, each representing 96 (3 × 32) PCM audio samples, and so there are 1152

Header	CRC	AUDIO data				AD
System 32 bits	Parity 16 bits	Allocation bits/SBS	Selection SCFSI	Scaling factors	Sub-band samples (SBS) (three portions of 12 sub-band samples each)	Ancillary data

- The header carries the synchronization and system information (see Table 3.1).
- The use of the parity (CRC) is optional.
- The 'bit allocation per SBS' field contains 32 integers coded on 2–4 bits depending on the sub-band, each of them defining the resolution for coding the samples of one of the 32 sub-bands and whether or not these sub-band samples are grouped in threes.
- The SCFSI (scale factor selection information) field indicates whether the scale factor is valid for the whole frame duration or whether there are two or three different scale factors.
- The 'scaling factors' field contains integers coded on 6 bits, each of them giving the multiplication factor of the samples of one sub-band for the portion of the frame defined by the SCFSI.

Fig. 3.27 Simplified representation of the MPEG audio layer II frame

samples in total. The duration is thus three times the duration of the layer I frame, i.e. 36 ms at 32 kHz, 26.1 ms at 44.1 kHz, 24 ms at 48 kHz. The audio part of the layer II frame differs from that of layer I, and its bit allocation is more complex due to the numerous coding options.

Note 3.1

A fourth type of image (D type) is foreseen by MPEG-1, which is very rough and simple to decode as it only uses the DC coefficient for coding. D pictures are mainly intended for browsing quickly inside a video sequence (e.g. for a picture search).

Note 3.2

The MPEG-2 audio standard includes all the features of MPEG-1, but adds some new extensions such as an MPEG-1 compatible multichannel sound mode (5 channel surround sound for instance), which is also foreseen in the DVB specifications). This compatibility is ensured by transmitting two main left and right channels compatible with the MPEG-1 standard and adding supplementary information in the 'ancillary_data' field which indicates in which extension packets (with different PID) the multichannel informations can be found. These extension data are simply ignored by a standard MPEG-1 decoder and processed only by an appropriate extension in the MPEG-2 decoder. The principle of compatible 'surround' encoding and decoding is illustrated in Fig. 3.28.

The MPEG-2 standard includes also the possibility of using sampling frequencies of half the standard values (16 kHz/22.05 kHz/24 kHz), which divide the required bit-rate by a factor of 2, but which also reduce the audio bandwidth in the same ratio.

Note 3.3

With layers I and II, only the 'intensity_stereo' mode of joint _stereo is allowed; layer III allows intensity_stereo and MS_stereo, and even a combination of both.

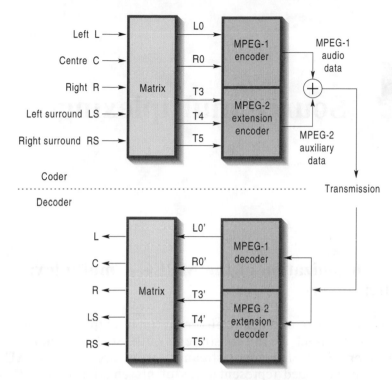

Fig. 3.28 Principle of MPEG-2 (MPEG-1 compatible) 'surround' encoding/decoding

4 Source multiplexing

4.1 Organization of the MPEG-1 multiplex: system layer

Audio and video encoders deliver as their output elementary streams (**ES**) which are the constituents of the so-called **compression layer**. Each elementary streams carries access units (**AU**) which are the coded representations of presentation units (**PU**), i.e. decoded pictures or audio frames depending on the nature of the elementary stream.

These bitstreams, as well as other streams carrying other *private data*, have to be combined in an organized manner and supplemented with additional information to allow their separation by the decoder, synchronization of picture and sound, and selection by the user of the particular components of interest. Part I (system) of ISO/IEC 11172 International Standard (MPEG-1) defines the rules governing the constitution of a **system layer** grouping *video*, *audio* and *private* data elementary streams into a single bitstream, as well as the constraints on the elementary streams necessary to allow their combination (optional *padding* streams are also foreseen, for instance, to obtain a constant bitrate).

The main basic functions of the system layer which surrounds (or 'packetizes') the compression layer are as follows:

- packetization and combination of multiple streams into one single bitstream;

- addition of time stamps on elementary streams for synchronization at playback;

- initialization and management of the buffers required to decode the elementary streams.

A complete MPEG-1 *system* encoding device therefore has to effect video and audio encoding, the multiplexing of these data, private data and the necessary information to synchronize the audio and video parts of the decoder, and to indicate the necessary resources required for decoding the MPEG-1 bitstream (such as the size of the buffers required for decoding individual elementary streams with a theoretical reference decoder known as system target decoder – **STD**).

Each elementary stream is cut into *packets* to form a packetized elementary stream (**PES**); a packet starts with a *packet header* followed by the elementary stream's data. Table 4.1 details the different fields of an MPEG-1 packet.

Table 4.1 Structure of the MPEG-1 packet

Field	Definition (comment)	No. of bits
Start_code_prefix	Start code (00 00 01 hex)	24
Stream_id	PES type (4 MSB) and number (4 LSB)	8
Packet_length	Length of the packet (number of bytes to follow these two)	16
Stuffing_bytes	Optional stuffing (value FF hex)	0 to 16×8
Bits '01'	Beginning of STD_buffer field	2
STD_buffer_scale	Buffer size unit (0 = 128 bytes, 1 = 1024 bytes)	1
STD_buffer_size	Buffer size (in multiples of 128 or 1024 bytes)	13
PTS (optional)	Presentation time stamp (4 code bits + 33 bits + 3 marker bits)	40
DTS (optional)	Decoding time stamp (same structure as PTS)	40
Packet_data_byte	Data (N = packet_length less the six following fields)	$N \times 8$

The packet header starts with a start code on 32 bits, the last eight of which indicate the type (audio, video, private) and the identification number of the elementary stream from which it comes. The header indicates then the packet length (in bytes, on 16 bits; hence a maximum length of 64 kbytes) and the buffer size required by the STD for decoding. It may also contain optional time stamps: a decoding time stamp (**DTS**) indicating the decoding time of the first access unit (AU) of the packet, and/or a presentation time stamp (**PTS**), indicating the time at which the corresponding presentation unit (PU) should be presented (displayed or made audible, depending on its nature). These time stamps are used for audio and video synchronization and are sent frequently (the standard specifies a maximum interval of 0.7 s between consecutive stamps of a PES). Time stamps are coded on 33 bits, which represent an absolute time expressed in periods of a 90 kHz reference clock (see also SCR and STC below).

A packet can carry a variable number of data bytes (within the 16 bit length limit), depending on the characteristics of the transmission or digital storage medium (**DSM**) for which it is destined. The standard also foresees the possibility of adding stuffing bytes to the packet (up to 16 bytes per packet), for instance to align on the physical sectors of a storage medium.

Packets are grouped in *packs*, the header of which contains timing and bit-rate information by means of the system clock reference (**SCR**) and mux_rate fields. The SCR field is used in the decoder to synchronize a 90 kHz system time clock (**STC**) common to all elementary streams, and which is used as a time base and measuring unit for the DTS and PTS time stamps sent in the packets. The pack header, which is detailed in Table 4.2, starts with a start code on 32 bits.

Table 4.2 Structure of the MPEG-1 pack header

Field	Definition (comment)	No. of bits
Pack_start_code	Start code (00 00 01 BA hex)	32
Bits '0010'	Beginning of SCR field	4
SCR[32 . . . 30]	System clock reference (4 MSB)	3
Marker_bit	Always 1	1
SCR [29 . . . 15]	System clock reference (15 intermediate bits	15
Marker_bit	Always 1	1
SCR [14 . . . 0]	System clock reference (15 LSB)	15
Marker_bit	Always 1	1
Marker_bit	Always 1	1
Mux_rate	MPEG multiplex bit-rate (in multiples of 50 bytes/s)	22
Marker_bit	Always 1	1

The first pack of an MPEG-1 system stream always starts with a pack header. The system header, detailed in Table 4.3, starts with

Table 4.3 Structure of the MPEG-1 system header

Field	Definition (comment)	No. of bits
System_header_start_code	Start code	32
Header_length	(Number of bytes to follow)	16
Marker_bit	Always 1	1
Rate_bound	Maximum bit-rate (mux_rate) in the sequence	22
Marker_bit	Always 1	1
Audio_bound	Number of audio PES in the bitstream (0–32)	6
Fixed_flag	Indicates fixed ('1') or variable ('0') bit-rate	1
CSPS_flag	'1' = bitstream uses the constrained parameter set	1
System_audio_lock_flag	'1' = harmonic relation between STC and audio $F_{sampling}$	1
System_video_lock_flag	'1' = harmonic relation between STC and frame frequency	1
Marker_bit	Always 1	1
Video_bound	Number of video PES in the bitstream (0–16)	5
Reserved_byte	Reserved for future extension	8
Stream_ID$_1$	Identification of first PES (type and number)	8
Bits '11'	Beginning of STD_buffer field	2
STD_buffer_bound_scale$_1$	Buffer size unit (0 = 128 bytes, 1 = 1024 bytes)	1
STD_buffer_size_bound$_1$	Buffer size (in multiples of 128 or 1024 bytes)	13
Stream_ID$_2$	Identification of second PES (type and number)	8
Bits '11'	Beginning of STD_buffer field	2
STD_buffer_bound_scale$_2$	Buffer size unit (0 = 128 bytes, 1 = 1024 bytes)	1
STD_buffer_size_bound$_2$	Buffer size (in multiples of 128 or 1024 bytes)	13
etc. . . . for $(n - 2)$ other PES	Idem for all PES (max: 16 video, 32 audio, 2 private)	$(n - 2)$ $\times$ 24

a start code on 32 bits. It is a special packet which delivers all the system parameters used during this stream (maximum bit-rate, identification of audio, video private data, minimum size of the input buffers, etc.). The system header can optionally be repeated at any new pack in the MPEG-1 stream in order to ease the access to a random point in the sequence.

The number of elementary streams in an MPEG-1 elementary stream is specified as follows:

- video, 0–16

- audio, 0–32

- private data, 0–2.

The MPEG-1 system stream ends with an 'end' code on 32 bits (00 00 01 B9 hex). Fig. 4.1 illustrates the content of a complete MPEG-1 stream.

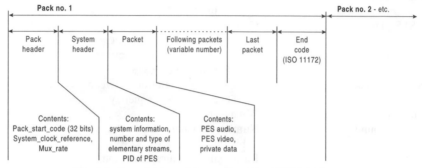

Fig. 4.1 Composition of the packs of an MPEG-1 bitstream

4.2   Organization of the MPEG-2 multiplex: program and transport streams

In the same way as for MPEG-1, MPEG-2 elementary streams (ES) are packetized in order to form the video, audio and private data PESs. As in the case of MPEG-1, packets from PES start with a packet header, the format of which is illustrated in Fig. 4.2 and detailed in Table 4.4 below.

The system part of MPEG-2 (ISO/IEC 13818-1), which defines the organization of the multiplex, foresees two different ways of multiplexing these PESs, in order to form two different kinds of bitstreams depending on the application. Fig. 4.3 illustrates schematically the way in which these two types of bitstreams are constructed.

Program stream

The MPEG-2 program stream is made up of one or more PESs (video, audio, private) which must necessarily share the same system time clock (STC). This type of stream is suitable for

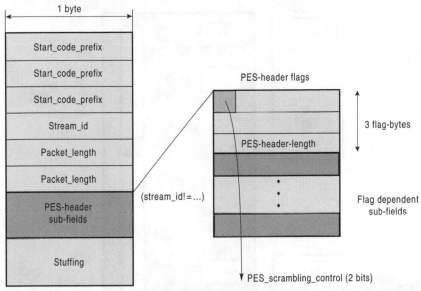

Fig. 4.2 Structure of the MPEG-2 PES header

Table 4.4 Structure of the MPEG-2 PES header

Field	Definition	No. of bits
Start_code_prefix	Start code (00 00 01 hex)	24
Stream_id	PES identification	8
Packet_length	Length of the packet (in bytes after these two)	16
PES_scrambling_control	Indicates whether PES is scrambled and control word number	2
Flags	Various flags	14
PES_header_length	Length of the remaining part of the PES ($x + y$)	8
PES_header_subfields	Variable field depending on flags	x bytes
Stuffing	Optional stuffing	y bytes

applications where the transmission channel or storage medium is supposed to introduce only a very low number of errors (bit error rate, **BER** $< 10^{-10}$). This type of medium is usually called *quasi error-free* (**QEF**). This is generally the case in multimedia applications based on CD-ROM or hard disk. In these cases, packets can be relatively long (e.g. 2048 bytes), and as the stream organization is similar to the MPEG-1 system stream, we will not discuss it here (see Section 3.1).

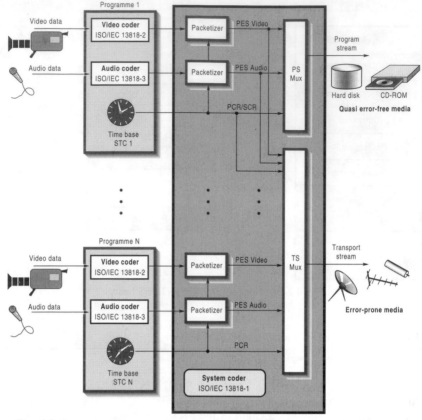

Fig. 4.3 Conceptual diagram of the generation of MPEG-2 transport and program streams

This kind of multiplex will most probably be used for storage of MPEG-2 video on the digital versatile disk (**DVD**), which will soon be available.

Transport stream

As its name implies, the MPEG-2 transport stream is primarily intended for the transport of TV programmes over long distances via transmission supports or in environments susceptible to the introduction of relatively high error rates (BER higher than 10^{-4}). These types of media are defined as *error-prone*.

In these cases, the packet length should be relatively short, in order to allow implementation of efficient correction algorithms, which will be detailed in Chapter 6. The length of the MPEG-2 **transport packet** therefore has been fixed to 188 bytes for the transmission of TV programmes via satellite, cable or terrestrial transmitters following the European DVB standard.

This type of stream can combine in the same multiplex many programmes which do not need to share a common system time clock (STC). However, the different PESs which make up a given programme have to use the same clock in order that the decoder can synchronize them. Fig. 4.4 illustrates the way in which the PESs that make up a transport stream are organized.

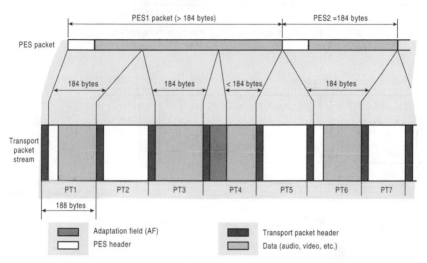

Fig. 4.4 Arrangement of the PESs that make up an MPEG-2 transport stream (PES1 is split between the transports packets PT1, PT3 and PT4; PES2 fits exactly into the transport packets PT6)

4.2.1 Composition of the MPEG-2 transport packet

A transport packet of 188 bytes is made up of a packet header of 4 bytes and a **payload** of up to 184 bytes, preceded by an optional *adaptation field* (see Fig. 4.5). In this context, the payload means the data from the PES composing the TV programmes, to which are added a certain number of data allowing the decoder to find its way in the MPEG-2 transport stream. The format of the transport packet header is illustrated in Fig. 4.6 and detailed in Table 4.5.

The ISO/IEC 13818-1 prescribes that a transport packet should carry only data coming from one PES packet, and that a PES packet should always start at the beginning of the payload part of a transport packet and end at the end of a transport packet (as shown in Fig. 4.4).

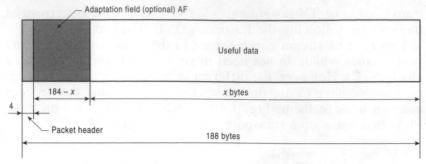

Fig. 4.5 Composition of the transport packet

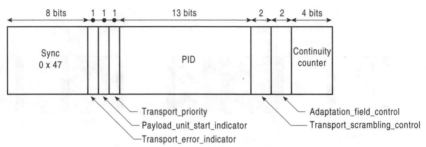

Fig. 4.6 Detail of the transport packet header

Table 4.5 Structure of the MPEG-2 transport packet header

Field	Definition (comment)	No. of bits
Sync_byte	Synchronization byte (1000 0111 = 47hex)	8
EI	Transport_error_indicator (indicates error from previous stages)	1
PUSI	Payload_unit_start_indicator (start of PES in the packet)	1
TPR	Transport_priority (priority indicator)	1
PID	Packet identifier (identifies the content of the packet)	13
SCR_flags	Transport_scrambling_flags (transport scrambling type)	2
AF	Adaptation_field_flag (presence of adaptation field in packet)	1
PF	Payload_flag (presence of payload data in the packet)	1
CC	Continuity_counter (between truncated PES portions)	4

As transport packets (188 bytes including 4 byte header) are generally (much) shorter than PES packets (e.g. 2048 bytes), PES packets will have to be divided into data blocks of 184 bytes. Since the length of PES packets is not generally an exact multiple of 184 bytes, the last transport packet carrying a PES packet will have to start with an adaptation field, the length of which will be equal to 184 bytes less the number of bytes remaining in the PES packet (Fig. 4.7).

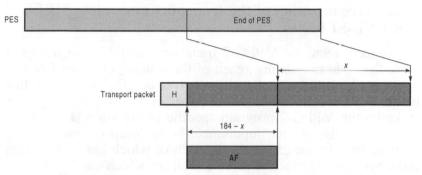

Fig. 4.7 Composition of the packet containing the end of a PES

In addition to this 'stuffing' function, the adaptation field will be used to carry various optional data and the program clock reference (**PCR**), which has the same role in an MPEG-2 program as the SCR has in an MPEG-1 system stream. The minimum repetition rate of the PCR is 10 times a second. In some cases, the payload of a transport packet can be solely composed of an adaptation field of 184 bytes (e.g. for the transport of private data). Fig. 4.8 illustrates the general format of the adaptation field, the content of which is detailed in Table 4.6.

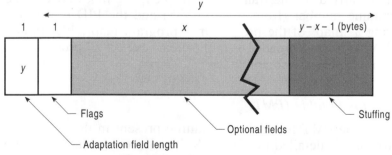

Fig. 4.8 Detail of the adaptation field

Table 4.6 Composition of the MPEG-2 adaptation field

Field	Definition	No. of bits
Adaptation_field_length	Total length $(y - 1)$ bytes	8
Flags	Information on the next field	8
Optional_fields	Optional data field (x bytes)	$x^* \times 8$
Stuffing	value FFh	$(y - 1 - x) \times 8$

4.2.2   Organization of the transport multiplex: MPEG-2 and DVB-SI tables

As we have seen, the MPEG-2 transport multiplex can transport more than one programme, each of them being composed of one or more PESs. In order that the receiver can find its way in this jungle, MPEG-2 has defined four types of tables, which together make up the MPEG-2 program specific information (**PSI**). Each table, depending on its importance, is made up of one or more *sections* (maximum 256 sections, each of which has a maximum 1024 bytes, except for the private sections which can be of up to 4096 bytes).

The repetition frequency of the tables is not specified by the standard, however it must be high enough (10–50 times per second) to allow the decoder to access quickly the required programme, e.g. in the case of a physical (RF) channel change.

The MPEG-2 tables

Program allocation table (PAT)

The presence of this table is mandatory, and it is carried by the packets of PID equal to zero (PID = 0×0000). Its structure is detailed in Table 4.7. Its purpose is to indicate, for each programme carried by the transport multiplex, the link between the programme number (from 0 to 65 535) and the PID of packets carrying a 'map' of the programme (program map table, PMT). The PAT is always broadcast 'in the clear' even if all programmes of the multiplex are scrambled.

Program map table (PMT)

There is one PMT for each programme present in the multiplex. Its structure is detailed in Table 4.8. It indicates (in the clear) the PID of the elementary streams making up the programme and,

Table 4.7 A section of the program allocation table (PAT)

Field (PAT)	Comment	No. of bits
Table-id (00)	Always 00 for the PAT	8
Section_syntax_indicator	Always 1	1
0	Always 0	1
Reserved		2
Section_length	Max. value 1021 (2 MSB = 0)	12
Transport_stream_id	Stream identification (in a network)	16
Reserved		2
Version_number	Incremented at every PAT change	5
Current_next_indicator	1 = current PAT, 0 = next	1
Section_number	Number of current section (1st = 00)	8
Last_section_number	Number of last section ($N_{tot}-1$)	8
Program number 0[a]	0 = network information table (NIT)	16
Reserved		3
Network_PID	PID of the NIT	13
Program_number 1	Programme number (1 = 1st prog.)	16
Reserved		3
Program_map_PID	PID of the (PMT)	13
. . . etc.	4 bytes per additional programme	. . .
CRC_32	CRC on 32 bits	32

[a] Program 0 (network information table, NIT) is optional.

optionally, other private information relating to the programme, which can eventually be scrambled (e.g. the ECM, which is one of the two pieces of information necessary for unscrambling programmes with conditional access, the other being the EMM carried by the CAT; see below and Chapter 5). The PMT can be transported by packets of arbitrary PID defined by the broadcaster and indicated in the PAT (except 0×0000 and 0×0001 which are reserved for PAT and CAT, respectively).

Conditional access table (CAT)

This table must be present as soon as at least one programme in the multiplex has conditional access. Table 4.9 details its structure. It is transported by the packets of PID = 0×0001 and indicates the PID of packets carrying the EMM for one (or more) conditional access systems.

Private tables

These tables carry private data, which are either in free format (see Table 4.10) or in a format similar to the CAT, except for the

Table 4.8 A section of the program map table (PMT)

Field (PMT)	Comment	No. of bits
Table_id (02)	Always 02 for the PMT	8
Section_syntax_indicator	Always 1	1
0	Always 0	1
Reserved		2
Section_length	Maximum value 1021 (2 MSB = 0)	12
Program_number	Prog. number (1 to 65 536)	16
Reserved		2
Version_number	Incremented at every PMT change	5
Current_next_indicator	1 = current PAT, 0 = next	1
Section_number	Always 00 (only one section)	8
Last_section_number		8
Reserved		3
PCR_PID	PID of program clock reference (PCR)	13
Reserved		4
Program_info_length	Length of the useful data (bytes)	12
Stream_type$_1$	Nature of elementary stream no. 1	8
Reserved		3
Elementary_PID$_1$	PID of elementary stream no. 1	13
Reserved		4
ES_info_length$_1$	N_1 = length of descriptors$_1$ field	12
Descriptors$_1$	Additional data	N_1 bytes
Stream_type$_2$	Nature of elementary stream no. 2	8
Reserved		3
Elementary_PID$_2$	PID of elementary stream no. 2	13
Reserved		4
ES_info_length$_2$	N_2 = length of descriptors$_2$ field	12
Descriptors$_2$	Additional data	N_2 bytes
. . . etc.	(ES no. x)	. . .
CRC_32	CRC on 32 bits	32

section length which can be as much as 4096 bytes, compared with 1024 for the other tables.

The additional DVB-SI tables

To the above MPEG-2 tables, the DVB standard adds complementary tables (service information, **DVB-SI**) which, among

Table 4.9 A section of the conditional access table (CAT)

Field (CAT)	Comment	No. of bits
Table_id (01)	Always 01 for the CAT	8
Section_syntax_indicator	Always 1	1
0	Always 0	1
Reserved		2
Section_length	Max. value 1021 (2 MSB = 0)	12
Reserved		16
Reserved		2
Version_number	Incremented at every CAT change	5
Current_next_indicator	1 = current PAT, 0 = next	1
Section_number	Number of current section (1 = 00)	8
Last_section_number	Number of last section ($N_{tot}-1$)	8
Descriptors	Access control data	Maximum 1012 bytes
CRC_32	CRC on 32 bits	32

Table 4.10 A private data section

Field (private)	Comment	No. of bits
Table_id	Any (except 00h to 3Fh and FFh)	8
Section_syntax_indicator	0 = free format, 1 = standard	1
Private_indicator	User-defined flag	1
Reserved		2
Private_section_length	Max. value 4093 (2 MSB = 1)	12
Private_data_byte[a]	Private user data	Maximum 4093 bytes

[a] The private data byte part is assumed here to be in free format (syntax_indicator = 0). If the syntax_indicator = 1, the format of this part is similar to the CAT (except length).

other things, allow the receiver to configure itself automatically and the user to 'navigate' by means of an electronic program guide (**EPG**) the numerous programmes and services available. DVB-SI is made up of four basic tables and three optional ones.

Basic tables

Network information table (NIT) This table, as its name implies, carries information specific to a network made up of more than one RF channel (and hence more than one transport stream), such as frequencies or channel numbers used by the network, which the receiver can use to configure itself for instance. This table is by definition the programme number 0 of the multiplex.

Service description table (SDT) This table lists the names and other parameters associated with each service in the multiplex.

Event information table (EIT) This table is used to transmit information relating to events occurring or going to occur in the current transport multiplex and even in other transport streams.

Time and date table (TDT) This table is used to update the internal real time clock of the set-top box.

Optional tables

Bouquet association table (BAT) This table can be used as a tool for grouping services that the set-top box may use to present the various services to the user, e.g. by way of the EPG. A given service or programme can be part of more than one bouquet.

Running status table (RST) This table is transmitted only once for a quick update of the status of one or more events at the time that this status changes, and not repeatedly as with the other tables.

Stuffing tables (ST) These tables are used, for example, to replace previously used tables which have become invalid.

Insertion of sections into the transport packets

Contrary to the PES, sections do not necessarily start at the beginning nor finish at the end of a transport packet. Whenever a section or a PES starts in a transport packet, the PUSI indicator (payload_unit_start_indicator) is set to 1. In the case of a section, the packet can start with the end of another section, whether or not it is preceded by an adaptation field (AF). In order to know where the new section starts, the first byte of the payload is a pointer_-field giving the offset of the beginning of the new section. This case is illustrated by Fig. 4.9, where a new section starts in a transport packet after an adaptation field and the end of a preceding section.

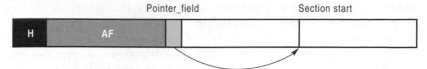

Fig. 4.9 Section start in a transport packet (general case)

4.2.3   Navigating an MPEG-2 multiplex

The following main steps have to be performed by the decoder in order to find a programme or a service in an MPEG-2 transport multiplex, once this multiplex is acquired, i.e. tuning to the RF channel is accomplished (in the case of a DVB compliant network, zapping within a network or bouquet would be eased by the DVB-SI information used to build the EPG) (see also Fig. 5.3):

1. As soon as the new channel is acquired (synchronization), the decoder must:

    (a) filter the PID 0 packets to acquire the PAT sections;

    (b) construct the PAT from the data of the sections;

    (c) present the available choice to the user (with DVB-SI, this choice could have been made before, if coming from a channel belonging to the same network or bouquet).

2. Once the user choice is made, the decoder must:

    (a) filter the PID corresponding to the PMT of this programme;

    (b) construct the PMT from the relevant sections;

    (c) filter the packet indicated by the PCR_PID field of the PMT, recover the PCR and synchronize the system clock (STC);

    (d) present the choices to the user, if there is more than one audio or video PID (assuming this choice has not previously been made by a user preference preset or through the EPG).

3. Once this choice has been made, the decoder must filter the PID corresponding to this choice.

The audio/video decoding can now start.

   The part of this process that is visible to users is the interactive presentation of the EPG associated with the network or bouquet, which can be built by means of the PSI and DVB-SI tables in order to allow them to navigate more easily the large number of programmes and services available.

However, zapping with digital TV is not as quick as with conventional analogue TV, as the synchronization process can be relatively long (1 s or more), due to the complex operations that have to be accomplished by the set-top box, i.e.:

- synchronization of the channel decoding part (only when changing the RF channel);

- acquisition of the PCR to synchronize the system clock of the MPEG-2 decoder;

- waiting for the next I picture to start real decoding (this alone can take up to 0.5 s).

5 Scrambling and conditional access

The proportion of free access programmes among analogue TV transmissions by cable or satellite is decreasing continuously, at the same time as their number increases; hence, it is almost certain that the vast majority of digital TV programmes will be pay-TV services, in order to recover as quickly as possible the high investments required to launch these services. Billing forms will be much more diversified (conventional subscription, pay per view, near video on demand) than what we know today, made easier by the high available bit-rate of the system and a 'return channel' (to the broadcaster or a bank) provided by a modem.

The DVB standard, as explained in the previous chapter, envisages the transmission of access control data carried by the conditional access table (CAT) and other private data packets indicated by the program map table (PMT). The standard also defines a common scrambling algorithm (**CSA**) for which the trade-off between cost and complexity has been chosen in order that piracy can be resisted for an appropriate length of time (of the same order as the expected lifetime of the system).

The conditional access (CA) itself is not defined by the standard, as most operators did not want a common system, everyone guarding jealously their own system for both commercial (management of the subscribers' data base) and security reasons (the more open the system, the more likely it is to be 'cracked' quickly). However, in order to avoid the problem of the subscriber who wishes to access networks using different conditional access systems having a stack of boxes (one set-top box per network), the DVB standard envisages the following two options:

1. **Simulcrypt**. This technique, which requires an agreement between networks using different conditional access systems but the same scrambling algorithm (for instance the CSA of the DVB), allows access to a given service or programme by any of the conditional access systems which are part of the agreement. In this case, the transport multiplex will have to carry the conditional access packets for each of the systems that can be used to access this programme.

2. **Multicrypt**. In this case, all the functions required for conditional access and descrambling are contained in a *detachable module* in a **PCMCIA** form factor which is inserted into the transport stream data path. This is done by means of a standardized interface (common interface, **DVB-CI**) which also includes the processor bus for information exchange between the module and the set-top box. The set-top box can have more than one DVB-CI slot, to allow connection of many conditional access modules. For each different conditional access and/or scrambling system required, the user can connect a module generally containing a smart card interface and a suitable descrambler.

The multicrypt approach has the advantage that it does not require agreements between networks, but it is more expensive to implement (cost of the connectors, housing of the modules, etc.). The DVB-CI connector may also be used for other purposes (data transfers for instance).

Only the future will tell us which of these options will be used in practice, and how it will be used.

5.1   Principles of the scrambling system in the DVB standard

Given the very delicate nature of this part of the standard, it is understandable that only its very general principles are available, implementation details only being accessible to network operators and equipment manufacturers under non-disclosure agreements.

The scrambling algorithm envisaged to resist attacks from hackers for as long as possible consists of a cipher with two layers, each palliating the weaknesses of the other:

- a *block layer* using blocks of 8 bytes (reverse cipher block chaining mode);

- a *stream layer* (pseudo-random byte generator).

The scrambling algorithm uses two control words (even and odd) alternated with a frequency of the order of 2 s in order to make the pirate's task more difficult. One of the two encrypted control words is transmitted in the entitlement control messages (**ECM**) during the period that the other one is in use, so that the control words have to be stored temporarily in the registers of the descrambling device. There is also a *default* control word (which could be used for free access scrambled transmission) but it is of little interest.

The DVB standard foresees the possibility of scrambling at two different levels (transport level and PES level) which cannot be used simultaneously.

Scrambling at the transport level

We have seen in the preceding chapter (Fig. 4.6) that the transport packet header includes a 2 bit field called 'transport_scrambling_ flags'. These bits are used to indicate whether the transport packet is scrambled and with which control word, according to Table 5.1 below.

Table 5.1 Meaning of transport_scrambling_flag bits

Transport_scrambling_flags	Meaning
00	No scrambling
01	Scrambling with the DEFAULT control word
10	Scrabling with the EVEN control word
11	Scrambling with the ODD control word

Scrambling at transport level is performed after multiplexing the whole payload of the transport packet, the PES at the input of the multiplexer being 'in the clear'. As a transport packet may only contain data coming from one PES, it is therefore possible to scramble at transport level all or only a part of the PES forming part of a programme of the multiplex.

Scrambling at the PES level

In this case, scrambling generally takes place at the source, before multiplexing, and its presence and control word are indicated by the 2 bit PES_scrambling_control in the PES packet header, the format of which is indicated in Fig. 4.4. Table 5.2 indicates the possible options.

Table 5.2 Meaning of PES_scrambling_control bits

PES_scrambling_control	Meaning
00	No scrambling
01	No scrambling
10	Scrambling with the EVEN control word
11	Scrambling with the ODD control word

The following limitations apply to scrambling at the PES level:

- the header itself is of course, not scrambled; the descrambling device knows where to start descrambling due to information contained in the PES_header length field, and where to stop due to the packet_length field;

- scrambling should be applied to 184 byte portions, and only the last transport packet may include an adaptation field;

- the PES packet header should not exceed 184 bytes, so that it will fit into one transport packet;

- the default scrambling word is not allowed in scrambling at the PES level.

5.2   Conditional access mechanisms

The information required for descrambling is transmitted in specific conditional access messages (**CAM**), which are of two types: entitlement control messages (ECM) and entitlement management messages (**EMM**). These messages are generated from three different types of input data:

- a *control_word*, which is used to initialize the descrambling sequence;

- a *service_key*, used to scramble the control word for a group of one or more users;

- a *user_key*, used for scrambling the service key.

ECM are a function of the control_word and the service_key, and are transmitted approximately every 2 s. EMM are a function of the service_key and the user_key, and are transmitted approximately every 10 s. The process for generating ECM and EMM is illustrated in Fig. 5.1

In the set-top box, the principle of decryption consists of recovering the service_key from the EMM and the user_key, contained

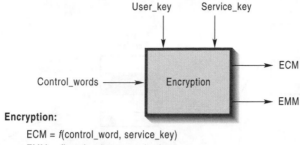

Encryption:

ECM = f(control_word, service_key)

EMM = f(service_key, user_key)

Fig. 5.1 Schematic illustration of the ECM and EMM generation process

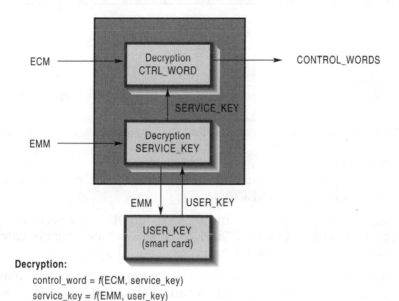

Decryption:

control_word = f(ECM, service_key)

service_key = f(EMM, user_key)

Fig. 5.2 Principle of decryption of the control words from the ECM and the EMM

for instance in a smart card. The service_key is then used to decrypt the ECM in order to recover the control_word allowing initialization of the descrambling device. Fig. 5.2 illustrates schematically the process for recovering control_words from the ECM and the EMM.

Fig. 5.3 illustrates the process followed to find the ECM and EMM required to descramble a given programme (here programme no. 3):

1. the program allocation table (PAT), rebuilt from sections in packets with PID = 0×0000, indicates the PID (M) of the packets carrying the program map table (PMT) sections;

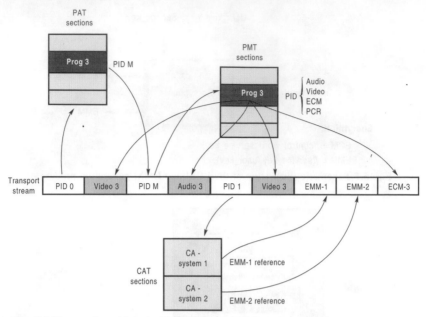

Fig. 5.3 Process by which the EMM and the ECM are found in the transport stream

2. the PMT indicates, in addition to the PID of the packets carrying the video and audio PESs and the PCR, the PID of packets carrying the ECM;

3. the conditional access table (CAT), rebuilt from sections in packets with PID = 0 × 0001, indicates which packets carry the EMM for one (or more) access control system(s);

4. from this information and the user_key contained in the smart card, the descrambling system can calculate the control_word required to descramble the next series of packets (PES or transport depending on the scrambling mode).

The above-described process is indeed very schematic; the support containing the user_key and the real implementation of the system can vary from an operator to another. The details of these systems are, of course, not in the public domain, but their principles are similar.

6 Channel coding (forward error correction)

Once the source coding operations have been performed (including multiplexing and eventually scrambling), a transport stream made of 188 byte packets is available for transmission to the end users via a radiofrequency link (satellite, cable, terrestrial network).

We previously indicated that these transmission channels are, unfortunately, not error-free, but rather error-prone due to a lot of disturbances which can combine with the useful signal (noise, interference, echoes). However, a digital TV signal, especially when almost all its redundancy has been removed, requires a very low bit error rate (BER) for good performance (BER of the order of 10^{-10}–10^{-12}, corresponding to 0.1–10 erroneous bits in 1 hour for a bit-rate of 30 Mb/s). A channel with such a low BER is called *quasi-error-free* (QEF).

It is therefore necessary to take preventive measures before modulation in order to allow detection and, as far as possible, correction in the receiver of most errors introduced by the physical transmission channel. These measures, the majority of which consist of reintroducing a *calculated* redundancy into the signal (which obviously reduces the efficiency of the source coding), are grouped under the terms 'forward error correction' (FEC) or 'channel coding' (this term often includes the modulation process). Such measures will of course depend on specificities of the physical transmission medium.

The *virtual channel* thus created between the input of the FEC encoder on the transmission side and the output of the FEC decoder on the receiver side is quasi-error-free and is sometimes referred to as a *super channel*.

Fig. 6.1 illustrates the successive steps of the forward error correction encoding process in the DVB standard. The terms *inner* coding and *outer* coding are seen from the point of view of the above-mentioned virtual channel. These steps are described in the following paragraphs, without going too deeply into the arcane world of the sophisticated error correction codes used, as this would require complex mathematical deviation. However, Appendix A explains the principle by describing some simpler codes, and the reader who is interested in more detail will find some references in the short bibliography at the end of the book.

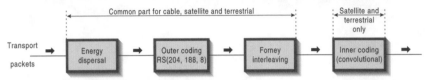

Fig. 6.1 The main steps of forward error correction on the transmitter side

6.1 Energy dispersal (randomizing)

Strictly speaking, this step is not part of the error correction process. However, the DVB requires that it should be undertaken before the correction process in order to obtain an evenly distributed energy within the RF channel.

Transport packets have a length of 188 bytes (see Fig. 6.2), the first of which is a synchronization byte of value 47_{hex} (01000111_{bin}), the MSB being transmitted first. In order to avoid long series of '0's or '1's, which would bring a DC content to the signal, the signal has to be randomized in order to ensure the energy dispersal in the channel. This is obtained by scrambling the signal by means of a pseudo-random binary sequence (**PRBS**) with the generator polynome $1 + X^{14} + X^{15}$. The diagram of the pseudo-random generator, which is the same for scrambling and descrambling, is quite simple and is shown in Fig. 6.3.

Fig. 6.2 The transport packet before error correction

The generator is re-initialized every eight transport packets by loading its register with the sequence 100101010000000. In order that the de-randomizer in the receiver can locate the beginning of

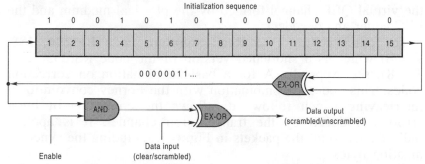

the sequence, the synchronizing byte of the first packet of the sequence is inverted (47_{hex} becomes $B8_{hex}$), the seven others remaining unchanged. In order that the synchronization bytes are not scrambled, the enable input remains inactive during that time, but the pseudo-random sequence is not interrupted. The energy dispersal device remains active even in the absence of a signal or with a non-MPEG-2 compliant stream as the input. Fig. 6.4 shows the transport packet sequence at the output of the energy dispersal circuit.

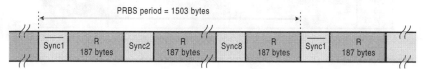

6.2 Reed–Solomon coding (outer coding)

In order to be able to correct most errors introduced by the physical transmission channel, it is necessary to introduce some form of redundancy allowing the detection and (up to a certain limit) correction of transmission errors to obtain a quasi-error-free (QEF) channel.

The first error correction coding layer, called *outer coding*, is used with all DVB specified transmission media; a second complementary layer, called *inner coding*, is used only in satellite and terrestrial transmissions (here 'inner' and 'outer' are relative to the virtual QEF channel formed by the physical medium and the FEC coder and decoder).

The outer coding is a **Reed–Solomon** code **RS(204, 188, T = 8)** which is a shortened version of the code RS(255, 239, T = 8); see Appendix A for a basic explanation on correction codes. This code, in combination with the Forney convolutional interleaving which follows it, allows the correction of burst errors introduced by the transmission channel. It is applied individually to all the packets in Fig. 6.4, including the synchronization bytes.

The RS(204, 188, T = 8) coding adds 16 *parity bytes* after the information bytes of the transport packets, which therefore become 204 bytes long; it can correct up to 8 erroneous bytes per packet. If there are more than 8 erroneous bytes in the packet, it will be indicated as erroneous and not correctible, and it is up to the rest of the circuitry to decide what to do with it. The overhead introduced by this efficient code is rather low (slightly more than 8% = 16/188). Fig. 6.5 indicates the format of the protected transport packets.

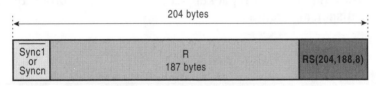

Fig. 6.5 A transport packet after Reed–Solomon coding

6.3   Forney convolutional interleaving (temporal spreading of errors)

The purpose of this step is to increase the efficiency of the Reed–Solomon coding by spreading over a longer time the burst errors introduced by the channel, which could otherwise exceed the correction capacity of the RS coding (8 bytes per packet). This process, known as Forney convolutional interleaving, is illustrated in Fig. 6.6.

L is the length of the packet to be protected (204 bytes) and I is the number of branches (here 12) of the interleaving and de-interleaving devices, called the *interleaving depth*. Hence $I = 12$ and $L = 204$. The interleaving device (in the transmitter) consists of a switched bank of 12 FIFOs (indexes $j = 0$–11) of length $M \times j$ (where $M = L/I = 204/12 = 17$), and the de-interleaving

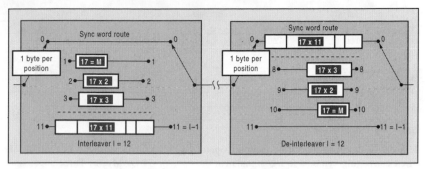

Fig. 6.6 Forney convolutional interleaving/de-interleaving (source: prETS 300 421).

device (in the receiver) consists of the same switched bank, but with FIFO lengths of $M \times (11-j)$. Thus, 12 successive bytes of index $j = 0$–11 will pass through the branch of the corresponding index, and each byte will be delayed, depending on its index, by 0, 17, 34, . . ., 187 positions (one position = one byte period) before transmission.

In the receiver, the same process happens simultaneously, and the byte delayed by $j \times 17$ positions at transmission will be delayed by $(11-j) \times 17$ positions, so that the delay is the same for all bytes, i.e. equal to $(j + 11 - j) \times 17 = 11 \times 17 = 187$ positions, and the initial order is recovered. However, a burst of errors affecting successive bytes in the physical channel will be spread by the de-interleaver over two successive packets, which will improve the efficiency of the RS coding and in most cases allow its correction. The synchronization byte always follows the branch of index $j = 0$.

Up to this point, the forward error correction (FEC) process has been the same for all RF transmission media envisaged by the DVB standard (satellite, cable, terrestrial). In the case of cable, the only remaining step before filtering and modulation (64-QAM, see Chapter 7) will be the conversion of the serial bitstream into two I and Q signals of 3 bits each, representing **symbols** of 6 bits. This purely logical operation is called *symbol mapping*. Fig. 6.7 represents this process schematically (the real process is more complex due to the differential modulation of the 2 MSBs of the 6 bit symbols; see Chapter 7).

For satellite and terrestrial transmissions, channel coding requires an additional step which aims mainly to reduce random error due to noise.

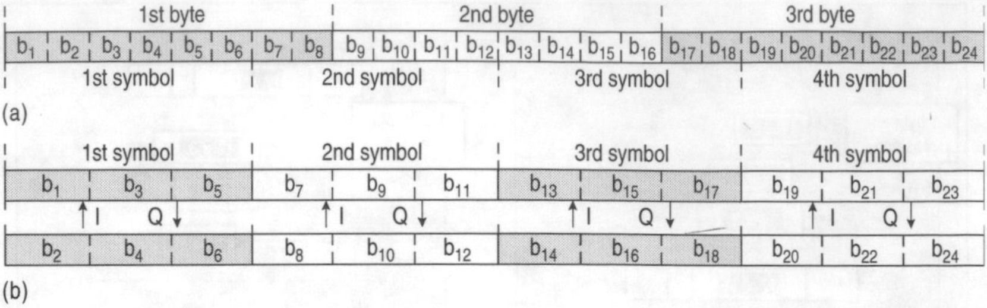

(a)

(b)

Fig. 6.7 Example of a possible mapping operation, first converting bytes to symbols and then converting symbols to I/Q signals (in the case of 64-QAM). (a) Three successive bytes form four successive 6 bit symbols (64-QAM); (b) 6 bit symbols are converted into I and Q signals (3 bits each)

6.4   Convolutional coding (inner coding)

The *inner coding* is a **convolutional coding** (see explanation in Appendix A) and is an efficient complement to the Reed–Solomon coding and Forney interleaving, as it corrects other kinds of errors. In the case of the DVB standard, the schematic diagram of the convolutional coder is illustrated in Fig. 6.8, and the basic parameters of the code are indicated in Table 6.1.

The strong redundancy introduced by the basic convolutional coding (100 per cent, as the convolutional encoder produces two output bitstreams, each with the same bit-rate as the input stream) allows a very powerful error correction. This can be necessary with a very low signal-to-noise ratio (SNR) at the input to the receiver, but it reduces by a factor of 2 the spectral efficiency of the channel. In this case, the X and Y output streams from the convolutional encoder are applied directly (after filtering) to the I and Q inputs of the QPSK modulator for a satellite transmission (see Chapter 7), and the useful bit-rate of the channel is half the transmitted bit-rate (which is what is meant by $R_c = 1/2$).

In this case, *symbol mapping* (2 bits/symbol for QPSK) is mixed with convolutional coding. However, this type of convolutional coding allows this redundancy to be lowered by means of **puncturing** the output of the convolutional encoder. This involves not taking all successive bits of the two X and Y output bitstreams, but only one of the two simultaneous bits with a certain *puncturing ratio*. The I and Q streams used for modulation are obtained by appropriately alternating the X and Y outputs in order to obtain two balanced bitstreams. In this way, it is possible to obtain the punctured code rates specified by the DVB standard ($R_c = 2/3$, 3/4, 5/6 or 7/8), which represent the ratio between the

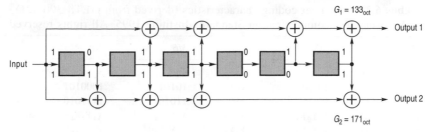

Fig. 6.8 Principle diagram of the DVB-S convolutional coder

Table 6.1 Basic parameters of the DVB convolutional code

Parameter	Abbreviation	Value
Code rate	R_c	1/2
Constraint length	K	7
First polynomial generator	G_1	171_{oct}
Second polynomial generator	G_2	133_{oct}
Free distance	d_{free}	10

useful (input) and transmitted (output) bit-rates. These R_c figures are obtained by multiplying the pure convolutional rate (1/2) by the inverse of the puncturing ratio (input bits/output bits). For instance, the code rate $R_c = 2/3$ is obtained with a puncturing ratio of 3/4 (2/3 = 1/2 × 4/3).

Puncturing increases the capacity of the transmission channel at the expense of a reduction of the free distance (d_{free}), which is a measure of the correction efficiency of the convolutional code. Given the power of the transponder and the size of the receiving antenna, the code rate chosen by the broadcaster will therefore be a trade-off between a useful bit-rate and the service area. Table 6.2 gives the free distance d_{free}, the puncturing scheme of X and Y outputs, and the sequence forming the bitstreams applied to the I and Q inputs of the QPSK modulator (in the case of satellite transmission) for the five code rates (R_c) specified by the DVB standard.

Table. 6.2 DVB inner coding characteristics (derived from prETS 300 421).

R_c	1/2	2/3	3/4	5/6	7/8
d_{free}	10	6	5	4	3
X	1	10 10	101	10101	1000101
Y	1	11 11	110	11010	1111010
I	X_1	$X_1Y_2Y_3$	X_1Y_2	$X_1Y_2Y_4$	$X_1Y_2Y_4Y_6$
Q	Y_1	$Y_1X_3Y_4$	Y_1X_3	$Y_1X_3X_5$	$Y_1Y_3X_5X_7$
S_{OFDM}	X_1Y_1	$X_1Y_1Y_2X_3Y_3Y_4$	$X_1Y_1Y_2X_3$	$X_1Y_1Y_2X_3Y_4X_5$	$X_1Y_1Y_2Y_3Y_4X_5Y_6X_7$

Notes
On lines X and Y, '0' denotes a suppressed bit, '1' denotes a transmitted bit.
For terrestrial transmissions based on OFDM modulation, additional steps are required after the inner coding: serialization of the bitstream, inner interleaving and symbol mapping to adapt the bitstream format to the high number of carriers used (see Chapter 7). The last line of the table, S_{OFDM}, represents the serialized bitstream (obtained by alternating I and Q lines) applied to the inner interleaving circuit used in the case of terrestrial OFDM transmission.

7 Modulation by digital signals

Once the source coding operations (MPEG audio and video coding, data insertion, multiplexing and eventually scrambling) and the channel coding (energy dispersal, outer RS coding, interleaving, inner convolutional coding) have been carried out, we have a data stream ready to be used for modulation of a carrier for transmission to the end users.

Depending on the medium (satellite, cable, terrestrial network), the bandwidth available for transmission depends on technical and administrative considerations, the latter largely depending on the former. In fact, technical conditions – particularly signal-to-noise ratio and echoes – vary considerably between signals coming from a satellite (weak but rather stable since they originate from a low power transmitter located more than 36 000 km away), those from a cable network (where signals are generally strong and stable at the subscriber plug) and those from a terrestrial transmitter where conditions can vary a great deal (especially in the case of mobile reception). As a result:

- for a *satellite* reception, the signal-to-noise ratio (carrier-to-noise ratio C/N or CNR) can be very small (10 db or less) but the signal practically does not suffer from echoes;

- by contrast, for *cable* reception, the SNR is quite strong (generally more than 30 dB), but the signal can be affected by echoes due to impedance mismatches in the network;

- in the case of *terrestrial* reception, conditions are more difficult, especially if mobile reception with very simple antennas is required (variable echoes due to multipath, interference, important signal level variations).

This is why modulation techniques have to be different, so that they can be optimized for the specific constraints of the transmission channel and for compatibility with existing analogue transmissions:

- on satellite, the channel width is generally between 27 and 36 MHz, because of the need to use frequency modulation (FM) for transmission of an analogue TV programme (bandwidth 6–8 MHz with associated sound carriers), due to the low CNR previously described;

- on cable or terrestrial networks, the channel width varies from 6 (USA) to 7 or 8 MHz (Europe) due to the use of AM with a vestigial sideband (**VSB**) for video and one or more audio carriers.

Digital transmissions will inherit this situation and will therefore generally have to use the same channel width as their analogue counterparts, so that, among other things, they can coexist with them on the same satellite, cable or terrestrial network and be compatible with existing transmission and distribution equipment. At the time of writing, only modulations for satellite and cable are fully normalized by the DVB project office. Terrestrial modulation is in the final phase of its standardization by ETSI; the basis of this standard is a bi-mode (2K/8K) **OFDM** (orthogonal frequency division multiplexing) modulation.

7.1   General discussion on the modulation of a carrier by digital signals

Digital signals are streams of rectangular pulses representing '0's and '1's. Depending on the channel characteristics, many bits can be combined to form symbols in order to increase the spectral efficiency of the modulation. However, without filtering, the frequency spectrum of digital signals is theoretically infinite, which would imply an infinite bandwidth for their transmission; this is, of course, not possible. As a result, appropriate filtering will be required to limit the required bandwidth; this filtering will have to be chosen in order to optimize the performance of the global transmission chain. Bandwidth limiting of a signal results in a theoretically infinite increase of its temporal response, which without special precautions would result in overlapping between successive symbols: this is called inter-symbol interference (**ISI**).

In order to avoid this problem, filtering should satisfy the first Nyquist criterion, in order that the temporal response presents zeroes at times which are multiples of the symbol period T. The most commonly used filter is called a *raised cosine filter* or, more simply, a Nyquist filter. In order to optimize the bandwidth occupation and the signal-to-noise ratio, filtering is shared equally between the transmitter and the receiver, each of which comprises a half-Nyquist filter (square-root-raised cosine filter). This filtering is characterized by its **roll-off factor**, α, which defines its steepness. Its frequency response is described in Table 7.1 (see also Fig. 7.1).

For a signal with a symbol period T (symbol frequency or **symbol rate** $1/T$) the bandwidth B occupied after Nyquist filtering with a roll-off α is given by the relation:

Table 7.1 Frequency response of the Nyquist filtering

Frequency	$0 < f < 0.5\,(1 - \alpha)$	$0.5(1 - \alpha) < f < 0.5\,(1 + \alpha)$	$0.5(1 + \alpha) < f < \infty$
Response	1	$0.5\{1 + \sin\,[\pi T(0.5 - f)/\alpha T]\}$	0

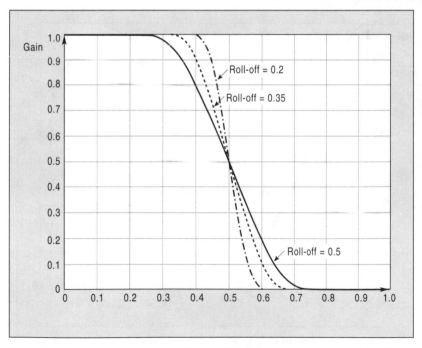

Fig. 7.1 Frequency response of the Nyquist filter for three values of the roll-off factor

$$B = (1 + \alpha) \times 1/2T$$

Fig. 7.1 shows the response curve of the Nyquist filtering (normalized to the symbol rate $1/T$) for three values of the roll-off factor (0.2, 0.35, 0.5), and Fig. 7.2 shows the corresponding temporal response (normalized to the symbol period T). The temporal response shows the presence of zeroes at instants that are multiples of the symbol period: in order to reduce the inter-symbol interference (ISI) to a minimum, the signal will have to be sampled at these instants with increasing accuracy as the roll-off decreases.

7.2   Quadrature modulations

In the simplest digital modulation schemes, the carrier is directly modulated by the bitstream representing the information to be transmitted, either in amplitude (**ASK**, amplitude shift keying) or in frequency (**FSK**, frequency shift keying). However, the low spectral efficiency of these modulations makes them inappropriate for the transmission of high bit-rates on channels with a bandwidth which is as small as possible.

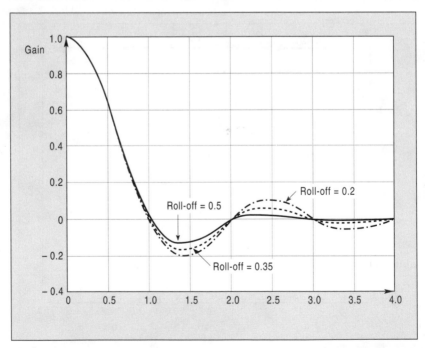

Fig 7.2 Temporal response of the Nyquist filter for three values of the roll-off ($\alpha = 0.2$, 0.35, 0.5)

In order to increase the spectral efficiency of the modulation process, different kinds of quadrature amplitude modulations (QAM) are used. These modulations were initially developed to transmit two independent analogue signals on one carrier (the first widely known application, developed at the end of the 1940s, is the modulation of the colour subcarrier of the NTSC system by the two colour difference signals).

Fig. 7.3 represents schematically the process of quadrature modulation and demodulation. Input symbols coded on n bits are converted into two signals I (in-phase) and Q (quadrature), each coded on $n/2$ bits, corresponding to $2^{n/2}$ states for each of the two signals. After digital-to-analogue conversion (**DAC**), the I signal modulates an output of the local oscillator and the Q signal modulates another output in quadrature with the first (out of phase by $\pi/2$). The result of this process can be represented as a **constellation** of points in the I, Q space, which represents the various values that I and Q can take. Table 7.2 gives the main characteristics and denomination of some quadrature modulation schemes as a function of the number of bits for each of the I and Q signals.

Figs 7.4 and 7.5 show, respectively, the constellations of **QPSK** modulation (quadrature phase shift keying or 4-QAM) and 64-QAM. These figures represent the situation at the output

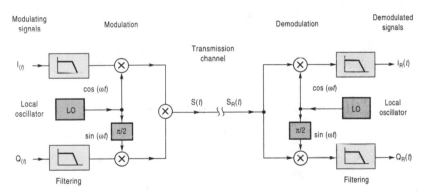

Fig. 7.3 The basic quadrature modulation/demodulation process

Table 7.2 Main characteristics of some quadrature modulations

I/Q coding (bits)	Bits/symbol	No. of states	Abbreviation
1	2	4	QPSK (= 4-QAM)
2	4	16	16-QAM
3	6	64	64-QAM
4	8	256	256-QAM

of the modulator, where each point is well distinguished from its neighbours, so that there is no ambiguity concerning the symbol value at this level.

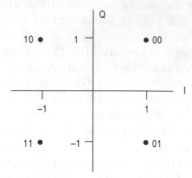

Fig. 7.4 Constellation of a QPSK signal

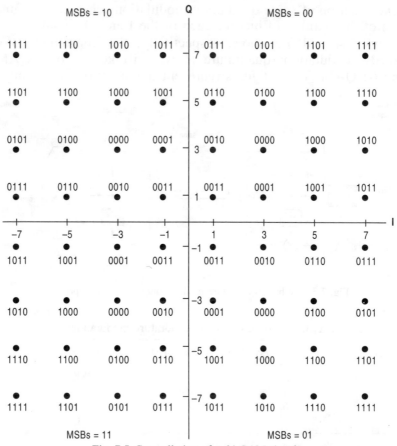

Fig. 7.5 Constellation of a 64-QAM signal

7.3 Modulation characteristics for cable and satellite digital TV broadcasting (DVB-C and DVB-S)

In order to make the best possible choice for these modulations, a number of theoretical studies and practical tests have been performed for cable as well as for satellite. Fig. 7.6 shows the theoretical bit error rate (BER) in ideal conditions for quadrature modulations from 4-QAM (QPSK) to 64-QAM as a function of the SNR ratio (see Note 7.1). One can see that, for a given bit error rate, QPSK has an advantage over 64-QAM of up to 12 dB.

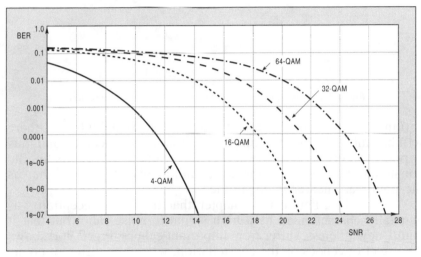

Fig. 7.6 Bit error rate (BER) as a function of signal-to-noise ratio (SNR) for various quadrature modulations

Taking into account the signal-to-noise ratio obtained on the receiving side, 2 bits/symbol (QPSK modulation) has been found to be the practical maximum, and therefore the best spectral efficiency, for satellite transmissions. In the case of cable, the signal-to-noise ratio is much higher, and a 64-QAM modulation (6 bits/symbol), roughly three times more efficient in spectral terms, can be used; some American proposals even use 256-QAM (8 bits/symbol).

Fig. 7.7 illustrates the effect of noise on the QPSK constellation recovered at the output of the receiver's demodulator in the case of a noisy satellite reception. Fig. 7.8 shows the case of a cable reception of a 64-QAM signal with a low signal-to-noise ratio (of the order of 23 dB). It is conceivable that, above a certain noise level, the demodulator will be unable to distinguish, with

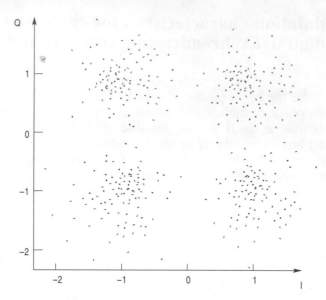

Fig. 7.7 A noisy QPSK constellation (weak satellite reception)

certainty, a point in the constellation from its neighbours; there will be ambiguity surrounding the symbol being received and thus a potential error. The greater is the number of points in the constellation, the lower the acceptable noise level will be, as the points are nearer to each other.

We stated earlier in this chapter that the cable reception was generally characterized by a high signal-to-noise ratio, but that it could, nevertheless, suffer from important echoes. Fig. 7.9(a) shows the effect of echoes on the constellation, where the different points cannot be distinguished because of a very high inter-symbol interference. The use of an appropriate echo equalizer in the receiver allows the recovery of an almost perfect constellation (Fig. 7.9(b)).

Other types of transmission disturbances or imperfections in the transmitting and receiving devices (imperfect frequency response, interference, intermodulation, etc.) increase the inter-symbol interference and appear as noise on the constellation, reinforcing the need for the error correction systems described in Chapter 6.

Another problem which the receiver has to cope with in the case of digital QAM modulations is that it does not have an absolute phase reference to demodulate the constellation (in contrast with NTSC or PAL subcarrier demodulation, where a reference burst is sent at the beginning of each line). For this reason, there is a phase ambiguity of 90° (the carrier recovery system can lock in four different phase states), which will prevent the receiver from synchronizing itself as long as the demodulation phase is incorrect.

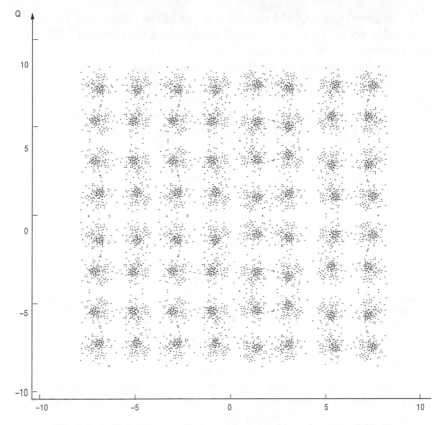

Fig. 7.8 A 64-QAM constellation with a signal-to-noise ratio of 23 dB

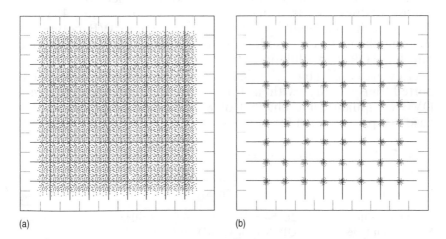

(a)   (b)

Fig. 7.9 (a) A 64-QAM constellation with significant echoes before echo equalizing.
(b) The same constellation after echo equalizing

In the case of the QAM modulation used for cable, this problem is avoided by using a differential modulation for the two MSBs of the symbol: the state of the MSB of I and Q corresponds to a phase change and not to an absolute phase state, which allows the receiver to operate in any of the four possible lock conditions (the constellation of the LSBs being identical in the four quadrants). Table 7.3 represents the truth table for differential coding of the MSB of the I and Q modulating signals used to generate the QAM employed in DVB-C.

Table 7.3 Truth table of the differential coding of the two MSBs in DVB-C

Symbol MSBs		MSB of I and Q		Phase change ($^\circ$)
B_{1T}	B_{2T}	I_T	Q_T	
0	0	I_{T-1}	Q_{T-1}	0
0	1	$\overline{Q_{T-1}}$	I_{T-1}	+90
1	0	Q_{T-1}	$\overline{I_{T-1}}$	−90
1	1	$\overline{I_{T-1}}$	$\overline{Q_{T-1}}$	180

B_{1T} and B_{2T} are the two MSBs of the transmitted symbol; I_T and Q_T are, respectively, the differentially encoded MSBs of I and Q for this symbol; I_{T-1} and Q_{T-1} are the MSBs of I and Q of the preceding symbol.

In the case of the (non-differential) QPSK modulation used for satellite, the 'out of synchronization' information can be used to modify (up to three times) the phase relation between the recovered carrier and the received signal until synchronization is obtained.

Taking into account all the above-mentioned considerations (and many others), the main characteristics retained for the DVB compliant digital TV transmissions are detailed in Table 7.4. Table 7.5 gives the maximum possible bit-rates on a DVB compliant satellite channel as a function of the channel width and the code rate for a QPSK modulation with $\alpha = 0.35$.

Grey areas in Table 7.5 indicate the cases which can be transported transparently (without transport stream modification) on a DVB compliant cable channel of 8 MHz with 64-QAM. In this case, the processing at the cable head-end will be limited to QPSK

Table 7.4 Main characteristics retained for DVB compliant digital TV transmissions

Parameter	Satellite (DVB-S)	Cable (DVB-C)
Channel width	26–54 MHz	8 MHz (7 MHz possible)
Modulation type	QPSK (= 4-QAM)	64, 32 or 16-QAM
Roll-off factor (α)	0.35	0.15

Table 7.5 Maximum bit-rates as a function of the channel width and the code rate (DVB-S) (derived from prETS 300 421, © European Telecommunication Standards Institute 1995. All rights reserved)

Channel width (MHz)	Maximum symbol rate (MHz)	Maximum useful bit-rate (Mb/s)				
		$R_c = 1/2$	$R_c = 2/3$	$R_c = 3/4$	$R_c = 5/6$	$R_c = 7/8$
54	42.2	38.9	51.8	58.3	64.8	68.0
46	35.9	33.1	44.2	49.7	55.2	58.0
40	31.2	28.8	38.4	43.2	48.0	50.4
36	28.1	25.9	34.6	38.9	43.2	45.4
33	25.8	23.8	31.7	35.6	39.6	41.6
30	23.4	21.6	28.8	32.4	36.0	37.8
27	21.1	19.4	25.0	29.2	32.4	34.0
26	20.3	18.7	25.0	28.1	31.2	32.8

demodulation, forward error correction (Viterbi decoding, de-interleaving, Reed–Solomon decoding, de-randomizing) in order to recover corrected 188 byte transport packets and to reapply a cable FEC (randomizing, Reed–Solomon coding, interleaving) before modulation (16 to 64-QAM).

A sample calculation of the spectral efficiency with parameters of DVB-S and DVB-C can be found in Appendix B.

7.4 OFDM modulation for terrestrial digital TV (DVB-T)

The European digital terrestrial television system (DVB-T) defined by the DVB is based on 2K/8K OFDM. It has been released by ETSI and published under the reference ETSI/EBU 300 744. The principle behind this type of modulation involves the distribution of a high rate bitstream over a high number of **orthogonal** carriers (from a few hundred up to a few thousand), each carrying a low bit-rate; the same principle was previously retained for the European digital radio system (Digital Audio Broadcast, DAB) which uses 2K OFDM. Its main advantage is its excellent behaviour in the case of multipath reception, which is common in terrestrial mobile or portable reception: in this case the delays of the indirect paths becomes much smaller than the symbol period.

OFDM modulation (orthogonal frequency division multiplexing) consists of modulating with symbols of duration T_s (in QPSK or QAM depending on the trade-off between bit-rate and robustness) a high number N, of carriers with a spacing of $1/T_s$ between two consecutive carriers. This determines the condition of

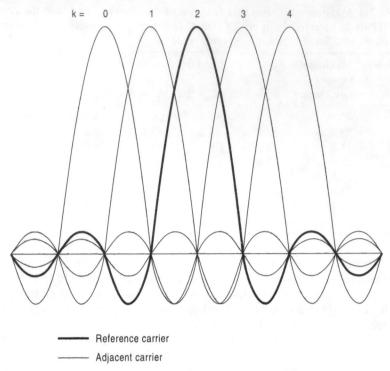

Fig. 7.10 Spectrum of adjacent carriers with OFDM modulation (source: *Revue de l'UER*, no. 224). © EBU/UER (August 1987)

orthogonality between the carriers, the spectrum of which can be seen in Fig. 7.10; for the central frequency of a given carrier, the spectrum of the carriers which surround it present a zero crossing.

The relationship between the frequency f_0 of the lowest carrier and that of carrier k ($0 < k < N - 1$), f_k, is given by $f_k = f_0 + k/T_s$. The frequency spectrum of such a set of carriers shows secondary parasitic lobes of width $1/T_s$, which can be seen in Fig. 7.11 (for $N = 32$ carriers).

However, in real terrestrial receiving conditions, signals coming from multiple indirect paths added to the direct path mean that the condition of orthogonality between carriers is no longer fulfilled, which results in inter-symbol interference. This problem can be circumvented by adding a guard interval Δ before the symbol period T_s in order to obtain a new symbol period $T'_s = \Delta + T_s$. This guard interval is generally equal to or less than $T_s/4$. The spectral density is modified by this guard interval, as can be seen on Fig. 7.12 (for $N = 32$ and $\Delta = T_s/4$), where a ripple in the useful band and a reduction of the secondary lobes

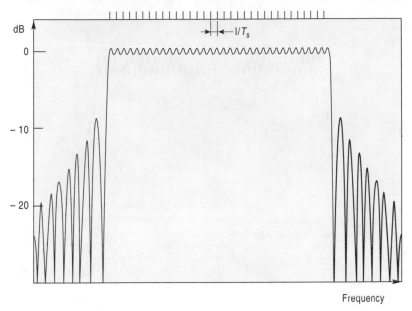

Fig. 7.11 Spectrum of an OFDM signal with 32 carriers (source: *Revue de l'UER*, no. 224). © EBU/UER (August 1987)

are observed. In general, N is much greater than 32, and the relative importance of the secondary lobes is much smaller than in Fig. 7.12; with the high values of N now defined for DVB-T (2048 or 8192), the frequency spectrum can be considered as virtually rectangular (Fig. 7.13).

Upon reception, a frequency conversion is made with the help of a local oscillator of frequency $f_0 + N/(2 \times T_s)$ (which is the value of the centre of the OFDM band) in order to obtain a frequency spectrum centred on 0 (zero IF) which is then sampled at N/T_s (double the maximum signal frequency). In practice, in order to simplify the filtering required to avoid any aliasing due to the sampling process, the useful bandwidth has to be less than half the sampling frequency; this can be done by removing some carriers at the two extremities of the RF band (for instance $N' = 28$ instead of $N = 32$). Further processing is carried out by means of a fast Fourier transform (FFT) on N points, which has to be performed within a time that is shorter than the symbol period T'_s.

For terrestrial digital television, the DVB system (DVB-T) is based on an OFDM modulation with 8192 (8K) or 2048 (2K) carriers, with the main characteristics shown in Table 7.6 (for a channel width of 8 MHz). In order to help the receiver to recover the signal and then to inform it about the modulation and channel coding parameters, the OFDM multiplex includes *continual pilot*

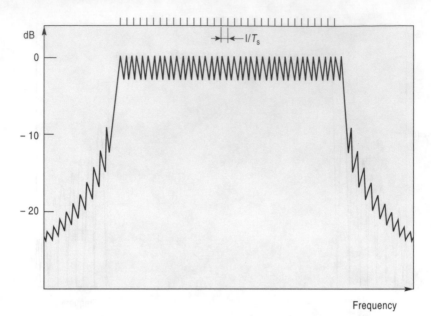

Fig. 7.12 Spectrum with a guard interval of $T_s/4$ (source: *Revue de l'UER*, no. 224). © EBU/UER (August 1987)

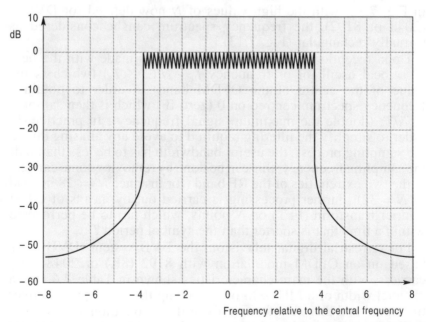

Fig. 7.13 Spectrum of a DVB-T channel with a guard interval of $T_s/4$ (8 or 2K OFDM)

carriers carrying **TPS** information (transmission parameter signalling), as well as *scattered pilot carriers* transmitted at twice the normal power level and modulated by a reference sequence.

The bitstream is split into successive frames of 104 symbols made up of as many bits as there are carriers in the multiplex (less the number of pilot carriers). Only 102 symbols carry useful data, as the first symbol of a frame is a *null* symbol (all carriers except the pilot are 'off') and the second is a reference symbol called a **CAZAC/M** (constant amplitude zero auto correlation) which carries the above-mentioned sequence.

The DVB-T proposal also includes options for hierarchical coding with a non-uniform QAM modulation, characterized by a bigger distance between the adjacent states of difference quadrants than between adjacent states in the same quadrant. This allows the simultaneous diffusion of a high priority bitstream modulating the two MSBs of a 16- or 64-QAM, which can then be considered as a robust QPSK modulated signal by a simple receiver, and a second bitstream with a lower priority modulating the remaining LSBs, which requires a more sophisticated but less robust QAM demodulation. This makes it possible to transmit in the same RF channel either independent programmes which can be received in different signal conditions, or the same programme with different picture resolution characteristics depending on the signal conditions and the complexity of the receiver. This could, for instance, allow low resolution mobile reception on simple small screen receivers and high resolution reception on fixed large screen sets. Fig. 7.14 shows an example of a non-uniform 16-QAM constellation.

The implementation of the 8K mode is rather complex, which makes the receiver costly, but its long symbol period (896 µs) used with the maximum guard interval (224 µs) allows a satisfactory reception even in the presence of very long multipath delays. This permits not only a good mobile reception but also the development

Table 7.6 Main parameters of the DVB-T system (2K/8K OFDM modulation)

Parameter	8K mode	2K mode
Effective carrier number (N')	6818	1706
Useful symbol duration (T_s)	896 µs	224 µs
Guard interval (Δ)	$T_s/4$ or $T_s/8$ or $T_s/32$	$T_s/4$ or $T_s/8$ or $T_s/32$
Consecutive carrier spacing ($1/T_s$)	1116 Hz	4464 Hz
Spacing between extreme carriers	7.61 MHz	7.62 MHz
Carrier modulation	QPSK or 16-QAM or 64-QAM	QPSK or 16-QAM or 64-QAM

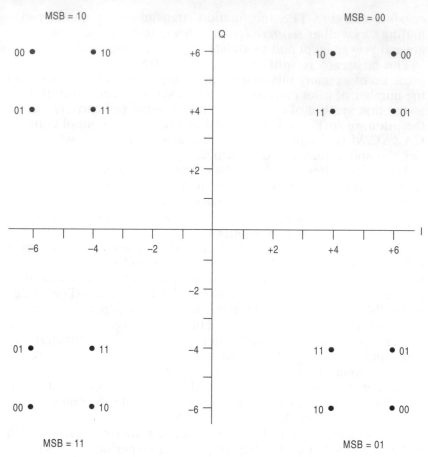

Fig. 7.14 Example of a non-uniform 16-QAM constellation

of broadcasting networks using a single channel on a wide area (so-called single frequency networks, **SFNs**) with transmitters that can be situated tens of kilometres from each other.

The 2K mode is simpler and the receiver is less expensive, but the shorter symbol period reduces substantially the performance in the presence of very long echoes, which practically makes it unsuited to single frequency networks. However, the implementation of a DVB-T receiver, even the 2K version, is more expensive than a QAM receiver with a reinforced forward error correction.

The first services of digital TV terrestrial transmissions will probably use the 2K mode of DVB-T for practical cost reasons (the UK is one of the first countries willing to start with DVB-T), and services starting later will be able to use the 8K mode when the cost of the components will be more affordable.

Note 7.1

The E_b/N_o ratio (average bit energy/noise density) is preferred over the C/N ratio (or CNR) for digital modulations, as it takes into account the number of states of the modulation. In fact, these two ratios, which describe the same physical reality, are related. E_b/N_o is related to E_s/N_o (average symbol energy/noise density) as follows:

$$E_b/N_o = E_s/N_o \log_2 M$$

where M represents the number of states of the modulation (e.g. four for QPSK, 64 for 64-QAM). E_s/N_o is itself related to C/N by the equation:

$$E_s/N_o = (C/N) \times B_{eq} \times T$$

where B_{eq} is the equivalent noise band ($\approx$ channel width BW) and T is the symbol period. From this comes the relationship between E_b/N_o and C/N (without FEC):

$$E_b/N_o \approx (C/N) \times BW \times T/\log_2 M$$

C/N and E_b/N_o are usually expressed in dB; this relation becomes then:

$$E_b/N_o \text{ (dB)} = \text{C/N (dB)} + 10 \log [BW \times T/\log_2 (M)]$$

In addition, it is referred to the symbol rate $R_s = 1/T$, so:

$$E_b/N_o \text{ (dB)} = \text{C/N (dB)} + 10 \log [BW/R_s \times \log_2 (M)]$$
$$\text{et C/N (dB)} = E_b/N_o \text{ (dB)} + 10 \log [R_s \times \log_2 (M)/BW]$$

In the case of satellite, M = 4 (QPSK); if BW = 33 MHz and R_s = 27.5 Ms/s, then:

$$\text{C/N} = E_b/N_o + 2.2 \text{ (dB)}$$

8 Reception of digital TV signals

8.1 Global view of the transmission/reception process

As a summary of the various concepts explained in the previous chapters, and as an introduction to the description of an integrated receiver decoder (IRD or more commonly set-top box), we will briefly and in simple terms review the various processing steps the TV signal has to follow from the source to the display on the end user's screen.

The upper portion of Fig. 8.1 (similar to Fig. 2.6) illustrates the steps on the transmission side, which has to deliver a multiplex of MPEG-2 programmes on one RF channel:

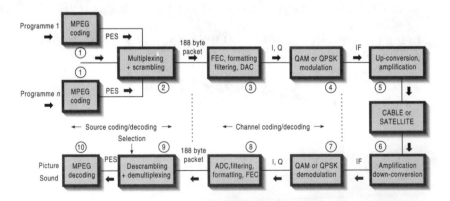

Fig. 8.1 The complete DVB transmission/reception chain

① Video and audio signals of the programmes to be broadcast are each put through an MPEG-2 encoder which delivers the video and audio PESs to the multiplexer (about four to eight programmes per RF channel depending on the parameters chosen for the encoding).

② These PESs are used by the multiplexer to form 188 byte transport packets, which are eventually scrambled (CAT tables carrying conditional access information ECM/EMM are inserted in this case), as well as the PAT, PMT, PSI and DVB-SI tables for the electronic program guide (EPG).

③ The RS error correction increases the packet length to 204 bytes; in the case of satellite, the convolutional coding further multiplies the bit-rate by a factor of between 1.14 (R_c = 7/8) and 2 (R_c = 1/2); formatting of the data (*symbol mapping*) followed by filtering and D/A conversion produce the I and Q analogue signals.

④ The I and Q signals modulate (QPSK for satellite and QAM for cable) an IF carrier (intermediate frequency of the order of 70 MHz).

⑤ This IF is up-converted into the appropriate frequency band (depending on the medium) for transmission to the end users.

In the case of satellite, the frequency change will bring it to the required value for the **uplink** to the satellite **transponder**, where it will again be frequency converted for diffusion to the end users in the KU band (from 10.7 to 12.75 GHz).

Direct diffusion by cable is relatively rare in Europe, and most of the time the process involves a satellite and a head-end station which ensures QPSK demodulation/QAM remodulation and transposition on the appropriate VHF or UHF channel.

The lower portion of Fig. 8.1 shows the complementary steps which take place on the receiver side; these are, in fact, the reverse of those on the transmission side:

⑥ In the case of satellite, an initial down-conversion takes place in the antenna head (low noise converter, **LNC**), which brings the frequency into the 950–2150 MHz range (input of the IRD), where it undergoes a second down-conversion (after RF channel selection) to an intermediate frequency that is usually 480 MHz. For cable, there is only one down-conversion from the VHF/UHF channel to an IF of 36.15 MHz in Europe.

⑦ The coherent demodulation of this IF delivers the I and Q analogue signals.

⑧ After A/D conversion, filtering and reformatting of I and Q (symbol demapping), the forward error correction recovers the transport packets of 188 bytes.

⑨ The demultiplexer selects the PES corresponding to the programme chosen by the user, which may previously have been descrambled with the help of the ECM, EMM and the user key (smart card).

⑩ The MPEG-2 decoder reconstructs the video and audio of the desired programme.

8.2   Composition of the integrated receiver decoder (IRD)

We have seen above the main steps in the digital TV transmission and reception processes, which indicate the basics of the IRD architecture. We will now go into a little more detail, without, however, going down to the level of electrical diagrams since this would offer little, due to their very great complexity. In fact, without even taking into account the cost of such an enterprise, it is practically out of the question for an individual to build their own IRD. In addition to the great difficulty associated with finding, assembling and testing the required components, even with the tools available to a clever electronic amateur (the main ICs can have more than 200 pins), the greatest difficulty is on the software side, which represents tens of man-years of work, involving very diverse specialities. Deep software layers are closely linked to the hardware, intermediate layers to the broadcast standard, and the highest layers to the network for which it is designed, and this is often partly defined by the broadcaster.

In addition, the technological evolution in this field is extremely rapid, in order to take advantage of the continuous progress of integration (the lifetime of a hardware generation will probably not exceed 1 year, with overlaps between generations in production). This is required in order to reduce, as quickly as possible, the cost of the digital IRD, which is currently much more expensive than its analogue predecessor, largely due to the cost of the memory required (fortunately, the cost of this memory has dropped a lot in recent months).

8.2.1 The satellite integrated receiver decoder

The block diagram in Fig. 8.2 represents the main functional blocks of a 1995/96 satellite IRD and their interconnection. It does not necessarily correspond to the partitioning used by all chip makers for manufacture of the ICs. This partitioning can vary substantially from supplier to supplier, and depends on the integration level, which increases quickly between two successive hardware generations.

The signals received from the satellite (frequencies ranging from 10.7 to 12.75 GHz; see Appendix C) are amplified and down-converted (in two bands) into the 950–2150 MHz range by the low noise converter (LNC) located at the antenna focus, and applied to the IRD's input.

Tuner

The tuner (sometimes called the 'front end'), generally controlled by an **I²C bus**, selects the required RF channel in the 950–2150 MHz range, converts it into a 480 MHz IF and achieves the required selection by means of a *surface acoustic wave filter* (SAW); the signal is amplified and coherently demodulated according to the 0° and 90° axes to obtain the analogue I and Q signals. Recovery of the carrier phase required for demodulation is carried out in combination with the next stages of the receiver which lock the phase and the frequency of the local oscillator by means of a carrier recovery loop. A block diagram of the digital satellite tuner is shown in Fig. 8.3.

Analogue-to-digital converter (ADC)

The ADC receives the analogue I and Q signals which it converts at twice the symbol frequency F_{SYMB} (of the order of 30 MHz in Europe). In most cases, this is done by means of a dual ADC with 6 bit resolution which has to work with a sampling frequency of more than 60 MHz. Here again, the sampling frequency is locked to the symbol frequency by means of a phase locked loop (clock recovery loop).

QPSK

The QPSK block, in addition to its functions of carrier and clock recovery loops mentioned before, carries out the half-Nyquist filtering complementary to that applied on the transmitter side

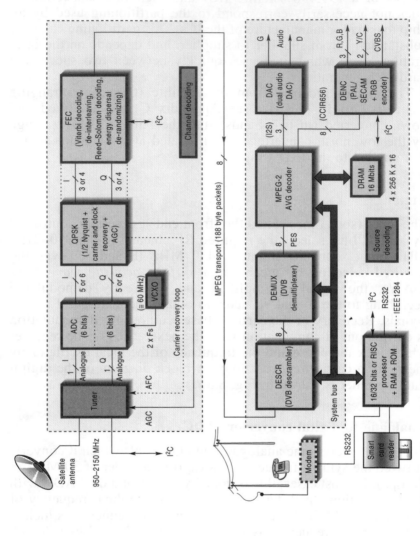

Fig. 8.2 Block diagram of a DVB satellite receiver (1995/96 generation) (the dotted lines represent functions which are sometimes combined)

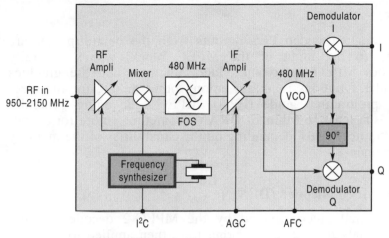

Fig. 8.3 Schematic of a satellite tuner (or front end)

to the I and Q signals. Digitized I and Q signals are delivered on
2 × 3 or 2 × 4 bits of the next functional block (FEC).

Forward error correction (FEC)

The FEC block distinguishes, by means of a majority logic, the
'0's from the '1's and achieves the complete error correction in
the following order: Viterbi decoding of the convolutional code,
de-interleaving, Reed–Solomon decoding and energy dispersal
de-randomizing; the output data are 188 byte transport packets
which are generally delivered in parallel form (8 bit data, clock
and control signals, of which one generally indicates uncorrect-
able errors).

Descrambler

The DESCR block receives the transport packets and communi-
cates with the main processor by a parallel bus to allow quick data
transfers. It selects and descrambles the packets of the required
programme under control of the conditional access device. This
function is sometimes combined with the demultiplexer.

Demultiplexer

The DEMUX selects, by means of programmable 'filters', the
PES packets corresponding to the programme chosen by the user.

MPEG

The audio and video PES outputs from the demultiplexer are applied to the input of the MPEG block, which generally combines MPEG audio and video functions and the graphics controller functions required, among other things, for the electronic programme guide (EPG). MPEG-2 decoding generally requires at least 16 Mbits of **DRAM** (sometimes more for decoding 625 line signals, depending on the capabilities of the memory management).

Digital video encoder (DENC)

Video signals reconstructed by the MPEG-2 decoder (digital YUV signals in CCIR 656 format) are then applied to a digital video encoder (DENC) which ensures their conversion into analogue RGB + sync. for the best possible quality of display on a TV set via the SCART/PERITEL plug and PAL, NTSC or SECAM (composite and/or Y/C) mainly for VCR recording purposes.

Digital-to-analogue converter (DAC)

Decompressed digital audio signals in I^2S format or similar are fed to a dual digital-to-analogue converter (DAC) with 16 bits or more resolution which delivers the analogue left and right signals.

Microprocessor

The whole system is controlled by a powerful 16/32 bit microprocessor (such as a 683xx or even a **RISC** processor), which controls all the circuitry, interprets user commands from the remote control, and manages the smart card reader(s) and the communication interfaces which are generally available. The software amounts to many hundreds of kilobytes, which are partly located in a **flash EPROM** in order to permit optional updates during the lifetime of the product (off air or via the communication ports).

Smart card readers

The conditional access device generally includes one or two of these (one might be for a banking card, for instance). In the case of a detachable conditional access module using the DVB-CI common interface (manifested in the shape of PCMCIA slots), the conditional access circuits and the descrambler are located in the detachable PCMCIA module. The demultiplexer integrated into the IRD receives the packets 'in the clear' (descrambled).

Communication ports

The IRD can communicate with the external world (PC, modem, etc.) by means of one or more communication ports. From the simplest (serial **RS232**) to the quickest (parallel **IEEE1284**), these ports, as well as a telephone line interface (via an integrated modem), are the necessary connection points required for inter-activity and access to new services (pay per view, teleshopping, access to networks).

8.2.2 The cable integrated receiver decoder

The block diagram for this IRD is shown in Fig. 8.4 and, in principle, differs from its satellite counterpart only in respect of the tuning, demodulation and channel decoding parts which are suited to the cable frequency bands (UHF/VHF) and the QAM modulation prescribed. We will therefore limit the description below to those blocks specific to the cable application.

Tuner

The tuner selects the desired channel in the cable band (VHF/UHF from 50 to 860 MHz), converts it into an IF frequency, F_{IF}, centred on 36.15 MHz, and achieves the appropriate selection by means of a SAW; after amplification, the IF signal is down-converted to the symbol frequency ($F_{SYMB} = 6.875$ MHz) by means of a mixer oscillator of which the frequency ($F_{OSC} = F_{IF} + F_{SYMB} = 43.025$ MHz) and phase are controlled by a carrier recovery loop from the following QAM demodulator. The cable tuner block diagram is shown in Fig. 8.5.

ADC

The transposed QAM signal is applied to an analogue-to-digital converter (ADC) with a resolution of 8 bits (up to 64-QAM) or 9 bits (up to 256-QAM) and converted with a sampling frequency generally equal to four times the symbol frequency F_s. The sampling frequency is locked to the symbol frequency by means of a clock recovery loop coming from the next block (QAM).

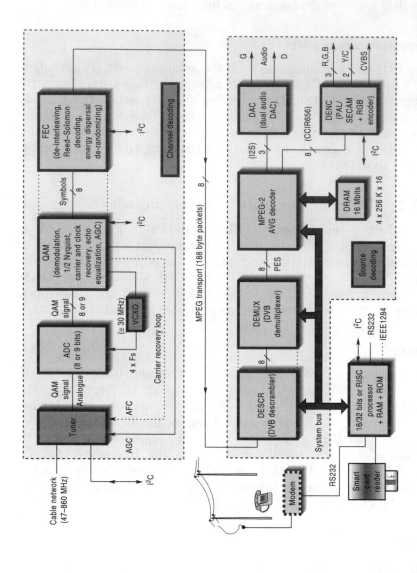

Fig. 8.4 Block diagram of a DVB cable receiver (1995/96 generation) (the dotted lines represent functions which are sometimes combined)

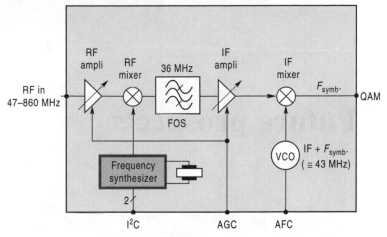

Fig. 8.5 Schematic of a cable tuner (or front end)

QAM

This is a key element in the channel decoding process: starting with the digital QAM signal, it performs digital demodulation and half-Nyquist filtering, echo equalization of the I and Q signals, and reformatting/demapping into an appropriate form for the FEC circuit (generally 8 bits parallel). It also plays a part in the clock and carrier recovery loops mentioned before, as well as generating the AGC for control of the IF and RF amplifiers at the front end.

FEC

The FEC block performs de-interleaving, Reed–Solomon decoding and energy dispersal de-randomizing; as is the case for satellite, the output data are the 188 byte transport packets in parallel form (8 bit data, clock and control signals).

Other functions

The processor, conditional access, descrambling, demultiplexing, MPEG-2 audio/video decoding and all other 'secondary' functions (OSD, IEEE1284, RS232, modem, etc.) are, in principle, identical to those described above for the satellite for the same level of functionality.

9 Future prospects

The fully digital era in consumer video applications is only just starting, and rapid and numerous changes in the services offered to the public are to be expected in the coming months. Due to the high investments required, it is understandable that these transmissions will start with pay TV services in nearly all countries.

However, even if the DVB standard has a powerful unifying role (27 countries had adopted the standard by mid-1996), in a very similar manner to that pioneered by the GSM standard for the mobile telephone some years ago, it could not impose a common conditional access control in the way GSM did at that time. As a result, a 'war of boxes' has already started between the various European and extra-European players, everyone trying to impose their technology in the field of conditional access and user interface (electronic program guide), and surprising alliances can sometimes be observed.

We will not, therefore, attempt to make any predictions in this field, as the risk of being contradicted by events taking place between the time of writing and the time of reading is far from negligible, and the person who could predict the winner would be very clever indeed. Nevertheless, we will try to list the main foreseeable technical changes in this field up to the turn of the century.

9.1   Terrestrial digital TV

Within Europe, the United Kingdom seems to be the first country willing to start a terrestrial service (as early as 1998, with the 2K variant of DVB-T). This new system would eventually replace the current PAL analogue transmissions after 10–15 years of coexistence between both systems.

One of the proposals for the transition period would consist of 'simulcasting' on the same RF channel of 8 MHz a digital version of each of the four or five existing analogue channels; in this case, one possibility would then be to stop transmitting the analogue versions, one channel at a time, over a period of 15 years or so.

This would allow the progressive freeing up of an important bandwidth, which could be reallocated either to new digital TV multiplexes to increase the number of programmes, or even to new bandwidth-hungry communication services. However, mainly for cost reasons, there has been some criticism of the OFDM modulation scheme, already adopted some years ago for the digital European radio system (Digital Audio Broadcasting, DAB). Its detractors would prefer a less robust but cheaper QAM scheme similar to the one used for DVB-C with a reinforced forward error correction.

A similar approach is envisaged in the USA, where the digital HDTV 'Grand Alliance' project had as one of its objectives the replacement of analogue NTSC transmissions in the year 2008. However, the choice of the modulation for terrestrial and cable will certainly differ from DVB, since it will probably be 8-VSB (8 states of AM modulation with a vestigial sideband). This is a kind of ASK modulation with more than two states, where one of the sidebands is almost completely removed by filtering in order to halve the required bandwidth for transmission.

As long as the technical and political choices for the replacement of analogue transmissions remain unclear, there is little chance that the digital TV decoders will be integrated into the TV set. As a first step, the sets integrating digital TV will probably be hybrid (capable of receiving analogue and digital transmissions), unless the 100% simulcast approach is chosen from the beginning.

9.2   Evolution of the set-top box

9.2.1   Functional integration

The diagram in Fig. 8.2 represents the functional partitioning of a European IRD of the first generation (available on the commercial market in the first half of 1996), and each of its functional blocks corresponds to a major integrated circuit.

Most of these ICs are fabricated with a C-MOS technology, with geometries of 0.6 or 0.5 μ. As a result of the very rapid progress of the IC technology, we will soon be able to group these functions in circuits with 0.35 μ geometries according to the possible following scheme:

- reduction of the (S)DRAM packages from four of 256 K × 16 to one of 1 M × 16;

- use of a RISC processor integrating a part of the external interfaces (IEEE1284 etc.);

- grouping of the transport stream processing (demultiplexer and descrambler functions) with the RISC processor or perhaps the MPEG-2 audio/video decoder;

- use of a monochip for channel decoding (for satellite as well as for cable), grouping the demodulator and the error correction, and possibly the input ADC(s).

By 1988–1989, in addition to the power supply, the tuner and the necessary memory, such a decoder (a block diagram of which is shown in Fig. 9.1) could consist of three main ICs:

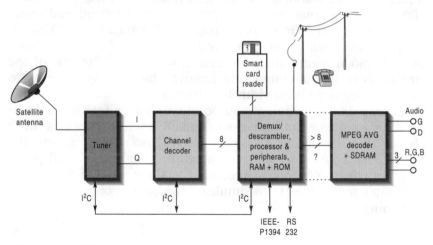

Fig. 9.1 Possible architecture of a DVB satellite receiver in 1997/1998 (dotted lines represent possible further integration options)

- channel decoder

- RISC processor with transport stream processing

- source decoder.

Integration will continue inexorably after this step, by the use of ever smaller geometries (0.25 μ or less), which will lead, well before the end of the century, to the integration of the source decoder and the PAL/RGB encoder with the microprocessor and transport stream processing. In addition, progress in the decoding algorithms and in memory management will make possible a reduction in the memory size required for decoding, which could then be shared with the processor, leaving more room for high resolution graphics for the EPG or other applications. In much less than 10 years, it is not unthinkable that all the active functions (processor, memory, channel and source decoding) will be integrated into one single 'super IC'. Only the power supply, a tuner, this super IC and a fair amount of software would then be required to build a set-top box.

9.2.2   Functional evolution of the decoder

In addition to the integration of the existing functions, which aims mainly to reduce the cost of the basic IRD, new functions will be added which will increase the appeal to the consumer, starting with the models at the expensive end of the market:

- Interfaces to the external world will evolve, and it is probable that the analogue PAL or SECAM output used mainly for recording will be enhanced (and later replaced) by a high speed digital I/O, for instance, for connection to a digital video recorder (the **IEEE1394** interface seems to be the preferred choice of some important manufacturers, and when introduced it could perhaps replace the current parallel interface, IEEE1284, which is used for data interchange with a PC).

- For IRDs connected to a cable network, which could become the preferred means of access to the 'information superhighway', a high speed *return channel* using the cable network instead of a simple telephone line will provide a much better interactivity, opening the door to completely new services. High speed Internet access could then be one of the possible value-added functions that could be integrated without major hardware modification to the set-top box. These new features of a digital TV set-top box are, among others, being defined and specified by the international Digital Audio Visual Council (**DAVC**).

- Among the list of new functions which could be added to the set-top box, the newly standardized DVD (digital video disk or digital versatile disk) is a high priority, as it could make use of the existing MPEG-2 decoder to realize, at relatively low cost, a combined IRD/DVD player (or even recorder) within the body of an existing VCR.

- Last, but not least, digital video broadcasting will ease the integration of TV and PC functions as techniques converge, and the new added functions will be more attractive due to the high data throughput offered by the transport channels. This will perhaps bring about the true home multimedia and multipurpose machine announced some years ago.

9.3   Other changes

9.3.1   The future MPEG-4 standard

Work continues within the MPEG group in order to elaborate new digital audio/video standards. The defunct MPEG-3, initially intended as the basis for a digital HDTV standard, was eventually included in the upper levels of MPEG-2. A new MPEG-4 committee has now been created, with the objective of defining a standard for audio/video coding at a very low bit-rate (from 10 kb/s to 1 Mb/s for moving pictures, and from 2 to 64 kb/s for the associated sound!).

This work is not, in principle, aimed at digital TV broadcasting, but at interactive multimedia applications at the interface between audio-visual and computer (radio)communications, such as videotelephony based on LAN, ISDN and standard telephone or radiotelephone networks. For these applications, MPEG-4 is going to define new coding principles, including being object oriented to ease editability and interactivity, and various scalability possibilities to allow easy adaption to a variety of transmission channel capacities.

The objective is to obtain an international standard by the end of 1998, which means that commercial applications based on MPEG-4 will not be available much before the year 2000.

9.3.2   New trends for signal processing

Despite the complexity of the algorithms used, the constant increase in the processing power of the new processors already allows purely software-based full-screen MPEG decoding in real time. Although this approach is definitely not economically attractive at present for a stand-alone set-top box, it is already of interest in some microcomputer based applications.

In recent years and months, new specialized processors have been developed which integrate a certain number of functional blocks dedicated to multimedia processing on top of a RISC or **VLIW** processor (audio, video and communication interfaces, motion estimators, variable length coder/decoder, etc.). These processors are generally used as dedicated multimedia coprocessors in a microcomputer environment, but specific derivatives will most probably appear for use as stand-alone processors, combining, for instance, all the control and decoding functions of an IRD.

The advantage of this approach is its very high flexibility, so that a well designed piece of hardware will be usable, by simple reprogramming, in very different applications (for instance, the same board could be used as a videoconferencing codec, an MPEG decoder or a music editing sytem, the only penalty to pay being the amount of memory required for the most demanding application).

In conclusion, we will have reached our goal at the end of this book if readers have acquired a (hopefully clear enough) global view of the new techniques used in digital television systems, which will perhaps give them the desire to investigate further this subject which is still in its infancy.

In order to satisfy the thirst for knowledge of interested readers, books much more dedicated to and specialized in particular aspects of this vast subject (including the new standards in preparation) will most probably be published in the coming months. The short bibliography given at the end provides some of the existing references.

Appendix A: error detection and correction in digital transmissions

From the very first digital data transmissions, the need to detect and, as far as possible, to correct errors introduced by the transmission link has been recognized. Various more or less complex solutions are used, depending on the characteristics of the link, but they invariably consist of adding a calculated redundancy to the original message.

A1.1   An error detecting code: the parity bit

The simplest means of detecting errors is the parity bit; it is still employed in short distance serial transmissions (for instance RS232), where it usually applies to words of 6–8 bits. On the transmission side, all the bits of the word to be transmitted are summed, and a supplementary 'parity' bit is added at the end of the word; this supplementary bit is equal to 0 if the sum of the bits is even, and 1 if the sum is odd (even parity), or the reverse (odd parity). On the reception side, the receiver does the same calculation and compares its result with the transmitted parity bit:

- if there is no error (or an even number of errors), the bits are identical;

- if there is one error (or an odd number of errors), the bits are different.

This system allows the detection, without being able to identify or correct it, of a 1 bit error in a word. The parity is only useful when the probability of more than one error per word is very low, as even numbers of errors are undetected, and when the communication link is bidirectional: in this case, the receiver which detects an error can ask the transmitter to retransmit the corrupted message. This principle of error correction is called *feedback error correction*.

A1.2 Block error correction codes

The block error correction codes apply to finite length words composed of k symbols (bits for instance) to which they add a calculated redundancy which increases the word's length to n symbols (bits in our example), so that $n > k$. The coding algorithm therefore adds $n - k$ bits (called control or parity bits) to the end of the original word, and the redundancy comes from the fact that only 2^k combinations out of the 2^n possible from the resulting code are used. The ratio k/n of the code (obviously < 1) is called the *yield* of the code.

In order to be able to distinguish between them in the case of an error, all elements of the code should be as 'distant' as possible from each other. The *Hamming distance* between two elements of a code is defined as the number of different bits situated in the same position. The *minimum* Hamming distance d of the code is defined as the number of different bits between any two elements of the code; one can demonstrate that the number, t, of correctible errors in a word is equal to $t = (d - 1)/2$.

The whole mechanism of the coding consists, therefore, of finding, for given n and d values (which define the correction capacity of the code), the coding algorithm giving the greatest k, and thus the best possible yield. This principle of error correction, which does not require a bidirectional link, is called *forward error correction* (FEC), by contrast to the preceding example (parity bit).

We will illustrate this principle by two simple codes (repetition and Hamming codes), in order to understand the philosophy of the more sophisticated codes used in digital video broadcasting (Reed–Solomon and convolutional codes) which we will not detail since they are based on rather complex mathematical concepts. The interested reader will, however, find some books entirely dedicated to these subjects in the bibliography.

A1.2.1   Repetition

One of the simplest means of correcting error transmissions is to repeat the bits of the message and to use a majority logic (*vote*) on the reception side to decide whether the received bit is a '1' or a '0' in the case of an error. For example, with a repetition factor of 3 ($k = 1$, $n = 3$), the coding of a bit would be:

Useful bit	Transmitted code
0	000
1	111

In the above example, the code is made up of two words of 3 bits, all of which are different; the minimum Hamming distance is therefore $d = 3$, and the correction capacity of the code is $t = (3 - 1)/2 = 1$ erroneous bit per word.

On the reception side, if we assume that the transmission channel does not introduce more than one error per word, a majority logic will be able to correct it by deciding, according to the table below, where the corrupted, albeit correctible, messages (one erroneous bit out of three) are in the shaded area:

Sent	000				111			
Received	000	001	010	100	011	101	110	111
Decoded	0	0	0	0	1	1	1	1

This type of error correction algorithm has a very low yield, as it triples the amount of information to be transmitted ($k/n = 0.33$), but it can correct high error rates (up to one bit out of three).

A1.2.2   The Hamming code (7, 4, d = 3)

This code applies to 4 bit words ($k = 4$, $2^4 = 16$ code elements) to which it adds 3 bits of redundancy (thus $n = 7$); therefore the yield is $k/n = 4/7 = 0.57$.

It is used for, among other things, the coding of critical parts of teletext magazines, and it works as follows. Let u be the original 4 bit words made up of the bits u_1, u_2, u_3, u_4. Let c be the resulting 7 bit code composed of bits u_1, u_2, u_3, u_4, v_1, v_2, v_3, obtained by means of the generating matrix **G** below:

	1	0	0	0	0	1	1
u_1	1	0	0	0	0	1	1
u_2	0	1	0	0	1	0	1
u_3	0	0	1	0	1	1	0
u_4	0	0	0	1	1	1	1
	u_1	u_2	u_3	u_4	v_1	v_2	v_3

The parity bits v_1, v_2, v_3 (situated in the shaded area of the matrix) obey the following relations:

$$v_1 = 0 + u_2 + u_3 + u_4$$
$$v_2 = u_1 + 0 + u_3 + u_4$$
$$v_3 = u_1 + u_2 + 0 + u_4$$

On the receiving side, the decoder receives the message y composed of bits u'_1, u'_2, u'_3, u'_4, v'_1, v'_2, v'_3, and does the same calculation as the encoder for the bits u'_1, u'_2, u'_3, u'_4, which yields the bits w_1, w_2, w_3:

$$w_1 = 0 + u'_2 + u'_3 + u'_4$$
$$w_2 = u'_1 + 0 + u'_3 + u'_4$$
$$w_3 = u'_1 + u'_2 + 0 + u'_4$$

The decoder calculates the *syndrome* $S = s_1$, s_2, $s_3 = v'_1 - w_1$, $v'_2 - w_2$, $v'_3 - w_3$. The syndrome's calculation can be represented by the parity control matrix **H** below:

0	1	1	1	1	0	0	s_1
1	0	1	1	0	1	0	s_2
1	1	0	1	0	0	1	s_3
u'_1	u'_2	u'_3	u'_4	v'_1	v'_2	v'_3	

If we assume that there is a maximum error of 1 bit per received word, the results will be as follows:

- if there is no error, the syndrome will be $S = 0, 0, 0$;

- if the bit u'_4 is erroneous, the 3 bits v'_1, v'_2, v'_3 will be wrong, and the syndrome will be $S = 1, 1, 1$;

- if 1 of the 3 bits u'_1, u'_2, u'_3 received is erroneous, two of the three relations used to calculate w_1, w_2, w_3 will be wrong (as each bit is used once in two of the three equations); the syndrome S will therefore have 2 bits at '1' and 1 bit at '0', the position of which will indicate which of bits u'_1, u'_2, u'_3 is in error;

- if the error affects a parity bit, its position will be indicated by the presence of only one '1' in the syndrome.

From this, it can be seen that this code allows the detection and correction of one error in the received word ($t = 1$) which corresponds to a minimum Hamming distance of $d = 3$.

A1.2.3   Reed–Solomon coding

This is also a block error correction code, the symbols of which are not bits but *finite field elements* (very often bytes); the mathematical theory of these codes can be found in specialized books, some of which can be found in the bibliography. We will therefore not present a theoretical description of the Reed–Solomon code, which would require long mathematical developments, but merely mention that it belongs to the cyclic class of codes and that it is a particular case of the so-called BCH codes (from their authors Bose, Ray-Chauduri, Hocquenghem).

Like the two previous codes seen before, it is characterized by the three parameters (n, k, t) which define the size of the blocks on which it acts and the number of errors that it can correct:

- n is the size (in symbols) of the block after coding;

- k is the size (in symbols) of the original block;

- t is the number of correctible symbols.

This code is well adapted to the correction of burst errors introduced by a transmission channel, which is why it has been chosen as the *outer coding* algorithm for all the variants of the DVB digital television standard, with a symbol size of 1 byte.

In the DVB case, the size of the original block is the transport packet ($k = 188$ bytes); the specified Reed–Solomon coding increases the block size by 16 bytes ($n = 204$ bytes), and the minimum Hamming distance is $d = 17$ bytes, which allows the correction of up to $(d - 1)/2 = 8$ erroneous bytes per block. This code is denoted RS(204, 188, $t = 8$), and its yield is $k/n = 188/204 = 0.92$. It is a shortened version of the RS(255, 239, $t = 8$) obtained at encoding by adding 51 null bytes before the 188 byte packets in order to form 239 byte blocks applied at the input of an RS(255, 239, $t = 8$) encoder. This coding adds 16 parity bytes to the end of the original blocks, thus forming new protected 255 byte blocks. After encoding, the first 51 null bytes added before coding are discarded, which gives the new protected transport packets of 204 bytes.

Decoding of the Reed–Solomon code uses a fast Fourier transform (FFT) to calculate the syndromes and a Euclidean algorithm to find the error evaluation and localization polynomials. Erroneous words are calculated by using the *Forney formula* and are corrected within the limit of a maximum of 8 bytes per block.

A1.3   Convolutional coding

We will not develop the theory of these codes either, which is quite complex and requires high level mathematical explanations, and will again refer the interested reader to some of the references in the bibliography.

This coding acts on blocks of indefinite length: in practice it will be a *continuous bitstream* of arbitrary length. It is sometimes improperly called 'Viterbi coding', from the name of the author of the decoding algorithm generally used. It is intended to correct random errors, most often as a complement to a block code.

The convolution coding transforms the input stream into n output streams (two in the case of Fig. A.1), thus adding redundancy to it. There can be as many branches in parallel as one wants, but the most common case has two. The incoming stream is applied to the input of a shift register which has intermediate outputs (taps) after each stage; the stream advances one stage in the shift register after each new incoming bit. The incoming stream is also applied to the input of the first modulo 2 adding machine of each branch, which receives the output of the first intermediate tap of the shift register at its other input. The output of this adding machine is applied to one of the inputs of the next adding machine, which receives the output of the next stage of the shift register at its other input, and so on. Some adding machines are omitted and are assigned a coefficient of '0', while those that are not omitted are given the coefficient '1'. Each branch is then described by the binary or octal number formed by the sequence

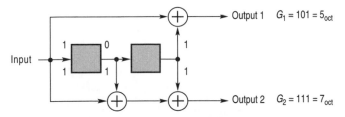

Fig. A.1 An example of convolutional coding producing two bitstreams ($R_c = 1/2$, $K = 3$, $d_{free} = 5$)

of '0's and '1's. Fig. A.1 illustrates the process for a simple case with two outputs X and Y and three taps.

The code is characterized by the following parameters:

- R_c, code rate: ratio between the input and output bit-rates (here 1/2)

- K, constraint length: number of usable taps (here 3)

- G_1, generator sum for X (here 101_{bin})

- G_2, generator sum for Y (here 111_{bin})

The generator sums G_1 and G_2 are obtained by assigning, from the left to the right, a '1' to the taps actually used and a '0' to the unused ones. The binary number obtained is generally represented in octal form (base 8). Hence, in the above example, the standard description is:

$$R_c = 1/2, \ K = 3, \ G_1 = 5_{oct}, \ G_2 = 7_{oct}$$

Another parameter, called the *free distance* (d_{free}), describes the correction capacity of the code: the higher the value of d_{free}, the more efficient is the correction (in the above example, $d_{free} = 5$).

The most standard method used to decode convolutional codes is based on the Viterbi algorithm, so named because of its inventor (1969). An explanation of the Viterbi algorithm would also be rather complex, and so we will simply indicate that its principle consists of finding the maximum likelihood route on a trellis representing the different possible states of the coder in order to find the most probable original message from the received stream.

Appendix B: spectral efficiency of cable and satellite transmissions with DVB parameters

The bandwidth occupied by an AM modulated signal is twice the bandwidth of the modulating signal, due to the two lateral bands generated by the modulation process. In the case of a digital signal of symbol period T which is Nyquist filtered with a roll-off α, the bandwidth will be:

$$BW = (1 + \alpha) \times 1/T$$

From this formula, we can now calculate the capacity of the channel and the spectral efficiency for various hypothetical cases:

Cable

With a roll-off $\alpha = 0.15$, a European channel of bandwidth $BW = 8$ MHz can accept a maximum symbol rate $F_s = 1/T = BW/(1 + \alpha) = 8/1.15 \cong 7$ MHz. A commonly used value is 6.875 MHz.

The usable order of QAM will depend on the network quality which determines E_b/N_o. In the worst case, 16-QAM (4 bits/symbol) will have to be used, resulting in a *brutto* bit-rate of:

$$R_b = 6.875 \times 4 = 27.5 \text{ Mb/s (without Reed–Solomon coding)}$$

Hence the brutto spectral efficiency will be 27.5/8 = 3.437 b/s per Hz. The *useful* bit-rate R_u is the product of R_b and the Reed–Solomon factor r_{RS} (188/204), and hence:

$$R_u = R_b \times r_{RS} = 27.5 \times 188/204 \cong 25.34 \text{ Mb/s}$$

The *useful spectral efficiency* is therefore 25.34/8 = 3.16 b/s per Hz.

In the best case, 64-QAM (6 bits/symbol) will be possible, resulting in a brutto bit-rate of:

$$R_b = 6.875 \times 6 = 41.25 \text{ Mb/s (without Reed–Solomon coding)}$$

Hence, the brutto spectral efficiency will be 41.25/8 = 5.156 b/s per Hz. The useful bit-rate R_u is calculated as before,

$$R_u = R_b \times r_{RS} = 41.25 \times 188/204 \cong 38.0 \text{ Mb/s}$$

The useful spectral efficiency is therefore 38.0/8 = 4.75 b/s per Hz.

Satellite

Theoretically with a roll-off $\alpha = 0.35$, a channel of $BW = 33$ MHz supports a maximum symbol rate $F_s = 1/T = BW/(1 + \alpha) = 33/1.35 = 24.4$ MHz.

With QPSK modulation (2 bits/symbol), the brutto bit-rate is therefore

$$R_b = 2 \times F_s = 48.88 \text{ Mb/s (without Reed–Solomon and inner codings)}$$

In practice, this capacity can be slightly higher (a ratio BW/F_s of 1.20 between bandwidth and symbol rates results in only a marginal degradation). The maximum symbol rate thus becomes 33/1.20 = 27.5 MHz; the brutto bit-rate $R_b = 55$ Mb/s and the brutto spectral efficiency is 55/33 = 1.66 b/s per Hz.

The useful bit-rate depends on the code rate r_c chosen for the inner coding; it is equal to the product of the brutto bit-rate R_b, r_c and r_{RS} (Reed–Solomon factor = 188/204). In the worst case (minimal E_b/N_o) the code rate $r_c = 1/2$ will have to be used to ensure a satisfactory service (BER < 10^{-10}); in this case the useful bit-rate is:

$$R_u = R_b \times r_c \times r_{RS} = 55 \times 1/2 \times 188/204 = 25.34 \text{ Mb/s}$$

The useful spectral efficiency is therefore 25.34/33 = 0.76 b/s per Hz.

In the best case (maximal E_b/N_o), the same service quality can be obtained with $r_c = 7/8$; the useful bit-rate becomes:

$$R_u = R_b \times r_c \times r_{RS} = 55 \times 7/8 \times 188/204 = 44.35 \text{ Mb/s}$$

The *useful* spectral efficiency is therefore 44.35/33 = 1.34 b/s per Hz.

In fact, most digital satellite TV transmissions in use today on ASTRA and EUTELSAT (33 MHz channels) use this maximum symbol rate of 27.5 MHz and a code rate $r_c = 3/4$. This corresponds to a useful bit rate of $27.5 \times 2 \times 3/4 \times 188/204 \simeq 38.0$ Mb/s, which allows transparent retransmission on a cable network with 8 MHz channels by using 64-QAM at a signal rate of 6.875 MHz (best case example in our calculation for cable above). In this case, the spectral efficiency of the satellite channel is 38.0/33 = 1.15 b/s per Hz.

Appendix C: reception of the new digital TV channels of ASTRA and EUTELSAT

The new digital satellites operate mainly in the so-called DBS band (11.7–12.5 GHz); this band has until now been used in circular polarization by high power satellites such as TDF 1/2, Hispasat, etc. At 19.2°E, ASTRA 1E and 1F provide 40 channels in the DBS band. These channels are 33 MHz wide and situated on a grid with a 19.5 MHz step. ASTRA 1G added 16 channels of 26 MHz on a grid of 14.75 MHz in the so-called 'Telecom' band (12.5 to 12.75 GHz).

Positioned on 28.2°E, the new ASTRA 2 family of satellites (used among others by BSkyB digital services) use the same channels.

The tables overleaf give the frequency allocation of the digital channels of ASTRA. EUTELSAT's 'Hot Birds' 2, 3 and 4 at 13E use the same frequency bands, but with different channels (33 MHz channels on an uniform grid of 19,18 MHz from 11.700 to 12.750 GHz).

A dozen (as yet unspecified) channels between 12.50 and 12.75 GHz (**FSS** band currently used by telecommunication satellites such as EUTELSAT, Kopernikus, Telecom) will be used later by ASTRA 1G and HOT BIRD 4.

In order to receive these new channels, ASTRA has specified a LNC (Low Noise Converter) or LNB covering the frequency range from 10.70 to 12.75 GHz in two bands, now called 'universal' LNB. The two bands are obtained by switching the local oscillator frequency by means of a 22 KHz signal superimposed on the LNC supply voltage; polarization is controlled, as is usual, by the value of the supply voltage (14V = vertical, 18V = horizontal):

- The low band (10.70–11.70 GHz) is, for the time being, almost exclusively used by analogue TV channels; it is converted into the 950–1950 MHz range by means of a 9.75 GHz local oscillator (22 kHz signal not active).

- The high band (11.70–12.75 GHz) is dedicated to the new digital TV broadcasts; it is converted into the 1100–2150

11.7–12.1 GHz (ASTRA 1E)				12.1–12.5 GHz (ASTRA 1F)			
Channel/ polarization	Frequency (MHz)	Channel/ polarization	Frequency (MHz)	Channel/ polarization	Frequency (MHz)	Channel/ polarization	Frequency (MHz)
65H	11 719.50	75H	11 914.50	85H	12 109.50	95H	12 304.50
66V	11 739.00	76V	11 934.00	86V	12 129.00	96V	12 324.00
67H	11 758.50	77H	11 953.50	87H	12 148.50	97H	12 343.50
68V	11 778.00	78V	11 973.00	88V	12 168.00	98V	12 363.00
69H	11 797.50	79H	11 992.50	89H	12 187.50	99H	12 382.50
70V	11 817.00	80V	12 012.00	90V	12 207.00	100V	12 402.00
71H	11 836.50	81H	12 031.50	91H	12 226.50	101H	12 421.50
72V	11 856.00	82V	12 051.00	92V	12 246.00	102V	12 441.00
73H	11 875.50	83H	12 070.50	93H	12 265.50	103H	12 460.50
74V	11 895.00	84V	12 090.00	94V	12 285.00	104V	12 480.00

12.5–12.75 GHz (ASTRA 1G)							
Channel/ polarization	Frequency (MHz)	Channel/ polarization	Frequency (MHz)	Channel/ polarization	Frequency (MHz)	Channel/ polarization	Frequency (MHz)
105H	12 515.25	109H	12 574.25	113H	12 633.25	117H	12 692.25
106V	12 522.00	110V	12 581.00	114V	12 640.00	118V	12 699.00
107H	12 544.75	111H	12 603.75	115H	12 662.75	119H	12 721.75
108V	112 551.50	112V	12 610.50	116V	12 669.50	120V	12 728.50

11.7–12.1 GHz (HOT BIRD 2)				12.1–12.5 GHz (HOT BIRD 3)			
Channel/ polarization	Frequency (MHz)	Channel/ polarization	Frequency (MHz)	Channel/ polarization	Frequency (MHz)	Channel/ polarization	Frequency (MHz)
50V	11 727.48	60V	11 919.28	70V	12 111.08	80V	12 302.88
51H	11 746.66	61H	11 938.46	71H	12 130.26	81H	12 322.06
52V	11 765.84	62V	11 957.64	72V	12 149.44	82V	12 341.24
53H	11 785.02	63H	11 976.82	73H	12 168.62	83H	12 360.42
54V	11 804.20	64V	11 996.00	74V	12 187.80	84V	12 379.60
55H	11 823.38	65H	12 015.18	75H	12 206.98	85H	12 398.78
56V	11 842.56	66V	12 034.36	76V	12 226.16	86V	12 417.96
57H	11 861.74	67H	12 053.54	77H	12 245.34	87H	12 437.14
58V	11 880.92	68V	12 072.72	78V	12 264.52	88V	12 465.91
59H	11 900.10	69H	12 091.90	79H	12 283.70	89H	12 475.50

12.5–12.75 GHz (Hot Bird 4)							
Channel/ polarization	Frequency (MHz)	Channel/ polarization	Frequency (MHz)	Channel/ polarization	Frequency (MHz)	Channel/ polarization	Frequency (MHz)
90V	12 519.84	93H	12 577.38	96V	12 634.92	99H	12 692.46
91H	12 539.02	94V	12 596.56	97H	12 654.10	100V	12 713.28
92V	12 558.20	95H	12 615.74	98V	12 673.28	101H	12 730.82

MHz range by means of a 10.60 GHz local oscillator (22 kHz signal activated). 10.60 GHz is left out of the low band in order to avoid any interference with analogue channels.

It should be noted that a good reception of digital TV signals requires an LNC with a local oscillator having better phase noise characteristics than has been required until now for analogue reception.

In order to allow more complex antenna switching functions, e.g. to receive two or more satellites, each transmitting in two bands, EUTELSAT has proposed, in cooperation with the receiver and antenna industries, an antenna control protocol via the coaxial cable:

- This proposal called **DiSEqC**™ (for Digital Satellite Equipment Control) is based on a modulation of the 22 KHz signal by digital messages. This will require a microcontroller in LNCs and switching devices for decoding and answering these messages as well as executing the corresponding commands.

- It is currently being examined for standardization by the ETSI and the IEC.

- If generalized, this system should allow an almost 'plug and play' connection of any receiver to any antenna system, all devices being identified by a unique address, and their functionality being readable by the receiver.

Appendix D: the main differences between the DVB-S and DSS® system

In the USA, high power Digital Broadcast Satellites (DBS) for 'direct to home' satellite broadcasting have been allocated a frequency band between 12.2 and 12.7 GHz. This band is divided into 32 channels of 24 MHz in circular polarization (16 channels left and 16 channels right), with a channel spacing of 27 MHz within the same polarization. Three orbital positions allowing full coverage of the USA, with 9° spacing for interference free reception with small dishes, have been allocated.

- 101° West, granted to DirecTV and USSB (U.S. Satellite Broadcasting) started in Spring 1994,

- 110° West, granted to MCI communications, due to start service late 1997.

- 119° West, granted to Echostar, which started service in Spring 1996.

The newcomers, Echostar and MCI, are or are expected to be compliant with DVB-S specifications. DirecTV and USSB use the DSS® (Digital Satellite System), historically the first 'direct to home' fully digital satellite TV broadcasting system in the world, and the most widespread in the USA. DirecTV and USSB offer together more than 200 TV programmes that can be received from almost anywhere in the USA with the same set-top box and a small dish of 18" (45 cm). They currently use three satellites named DBS-1, DBS-2 and DBS-3 and are copositioned at 101° West. A fourth satellite (DBS-4) is planned. Each satellite can be used either with 16 active transponders of 120 watts or 8 active transponders of 240 watts. In order to obtain similar coverages with the same receiving antenna size, the inner coding (convolutional rate) can be adapted to the power mode used.

Even if the same basic principles apply to both systems, DVB-S is an open system, whereas DSS® is a proprietary system of Hughes Electronics Corporation, of which the detailed specifications are therefore not available to the general public. Furthermore, since it was defined before the finalization of the MPEG-2 and DVB specifications, it started using MPEG-1 but is now mostly using MPEG-2 (at 544 × 480 pixels, a video coding scheme sometimes called 'MPEG-1.5'). Like DVB, audio coding of DSS® is MPEG-1, layer II. Other specifications of DSS® are generally simpler than those of DVB, since they were not intended to be medium independant, but restricted to satellite broadcasting.

Table D.1 gives the main differences between the most important technical features of DVB-S and DSS® systems, for reference only.

Table D.1

Feature or parameter	DVB-S	DSS®
Video coding	MPEG-2 (MPL@ML)	MPEG-1/MPEG-2
Audio coding	MPEG-1 layer II	MPEG-1 layer II
Multiplexing	Complex	Simpler
Scrambling	DVB-CSA	Proprietary
Transport packet length	188 bytes	130 bytes
Of which header	4 bytes[1]	3 bytes
Of which payload	184 bytes	127 bytes
Energy dispersal	$1 + X^{14} + X^{15}$	Not applied
Outer coding	RS(204,188, t=8)	RS(146,130, t=8)
Interleaving	Forney 12	Ramsey 13
Protected packet length	204 bytes	147 bytes[2]
Inner coding rates (R_c)	1/2, 2/3, 3/4, 5/6, 7/8	2/3 or 6/7
Symbol rate	Variable	Fixed $\cong$ 20 Ms/s
Roll-off factor	35%	20%
Modulation	QPSK	QPSK
Channel bandwidth	Variable	24 MHz

[1] Including sync byte.
[2] A sync byte (1Dh) is appended in front of each packet after RS coding and interleaving.

Appendix E: the IEEE1394 high speed serial AV interconnection bus

Interconnection of new digital audiovisual consumer equipment such as an IRD, a VCR, a camcorder and a multimedia computer will soon require a high speed link between the different pieces of equipment. As the equipment will be operating in a consumer environment, it has to be designed to be low cost and as easy to use as possible ('plug and play' with 'hot plugging' capability).

The recently standardized IEEE1394 (1995) high speed serial bus fulfils these requirements. It is based on Apple computer's 'FireWire' bus and allows communication at up to 400 Mb/s (an upgrade to more than 1 Gb/s is under study). Three standard speeds are defined (100, 200 and 400 Mb/s), but most current implementations only cover the first two speeds.

The IEEE1394 bus architecture enables the construction of a kind of network, made up of multiple (up to 63) participants called **nodes**. Each of the nodes has three basic functional components:

- a physical layer interface (PHY) which carries out the physical interfacing to the cable, bus arbitration and an active repeater function;

- a link layer controller (LINK) which assembles/disassembles data packets and handles handshaking and acknowledgement;

- a host controller (MCU) which deals with the higher levels of the bus protocols.

Fig. E.1 shows an example of a three node IEEE1394 network where the three above-mentioned components can be seen.

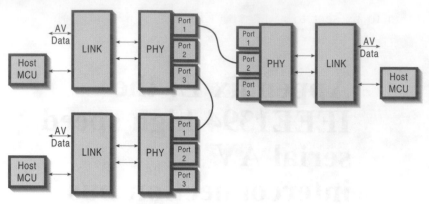

Fig. E.1 Structure of an IEEE1394 network (example with three nodes)

In the first implementation of IEEE1394 chipsets, the blocks denoted 'LINK' and 'PHY' generally correspond to two different integrated circuits. The IEEE1394 specification defines two kinds of data transfer which can coexist on the bus:

- **Isochronous** transfers are reserved for time-critical data, such as audio and video streams which need to be 'real time', as delays in audio or video frames cannot be tolerated. These types of transfer are allocated a guaranteed bandwidth and use time division multiplexing.

- **Asynchronous** transfers are reserved for non-time-critical data, which are used, for instance, for data interchange or storage and employ a more conventional process of handshaking and acknowledgement.

The proportion of bus bandwidth reserved for isochronous data packets is defined during the initialization phase by electing as the 'root node' a node which includes an isochronous resource manager (IRM). The IRM is then responsible for allocating isochronous resources for a whole session, based on 125 μs cycles on the bus. However, this is not sufficient to guarantee the very low jitter required to transmit, for example, an MPEG-2 transport stream over the bus (a variation in transport delay of less than 500 ns is required in this case).

In the case of a DVB set-top box, the AV data interface of the link circuit in Fig. E.1 would be connected to the transport stream path (i.e. between the output of the channel decoding part and the input of the source decoding part, before or after descrambling). This would allow, for example, the non-descrambled transport stream to be sent to a digital VCR, and in this case playback would require suitable access rights for viewing.

In order to enable the receiver to compensate for the delays introduced by the bus, an AV layer has been defined and standardized in the IEC1883 specification. It adds a 32 bit header (a quadlet in IEEE1394 terminology) to the 188 byte MPEG-2 packets which then become 192 bytes long, the header quadlet containing a time stamp which allows resynchronization at the receiving end. In addition, if a 192 byte packet (= 48 quadlets) cannot be transmitted in one 125 μs cycle, the AV layer allows it to be split into two, four or eight smaller equal parts (or blocks) which then can fit within one cycle.

Electrically, the bus is made up of two signals (DATA and STROBE), which are both transported in differential mode at low impedance on a shielded pair of conductors. An optional third pair is used for power distribution over the bus. Each branch of the network between two nodes can be up to 4.5 m long and is terminated at both ends by two 56 Ω resistors connected to a common DC reference. A low cost six pin connector (similar to those used on Nintendo Game Boy® consoles) and a specific cable have been standardized (see Fig. E.2). A version of the bus with only two pairs (without the power pair) has also been standardized.

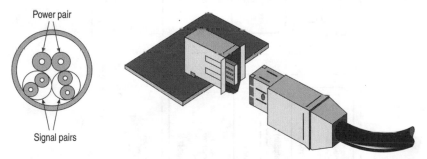

Fig. E.2 Cable and connector for IEEE1394 cabling (six pin version with power)

Appendix F: 1996/1997 DVB chipset for Satellite or Cable set-top boxes

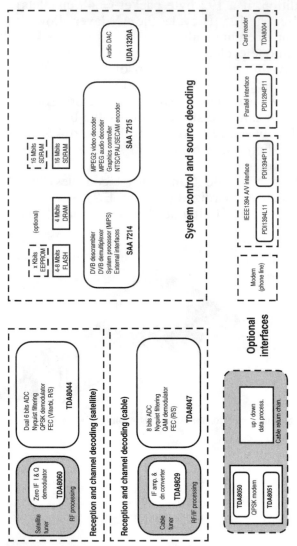

Fig. F.1 Example of a 1996/1997 DVB chipset for Satellite or Cable set-top boxes
(Source: PHILIPS Semiconductors)

Glossary of abbreviations, words and expressions

Abbreviations

AC-3 – multichannel digital audio system developed by the US company Dolby®.

ADC – analogue-to-digital converter (device converting an analogue voltage into a binary number).

AF – adaptation field (data field used to adapt the PES to transport packet length).

ASK – amplitude shift keying (digital amplitude modulation with two states).

AU – access unit (MPEG coded representation of a presentation unit: picture or sound frame).

B – bidirectional (picture): MPEG picture coded from the preceding and the following picture.

BAT – bouquet association table (optional table of DVB-SI).

BER – bit error rate (ratio of the number of erroneous bits to the total number of bits transmitted).

CA – conditional access (system allowing to limit the access to pay TV broadcasts).

CAM – conditional access message (specific messages for conditional access: ECM and EMM).

CAT – conditional access table (MPEG-2 table indicating the PID of conditional access packets).

CAZAC/M – constant amplitude zero auto correlation (reference symbol in the DVB-T proposal).

CCIR – Comité Consultatif International de Radiodiffusion (now IUT-R).

CCIR-601 (ITU-R 601) – recommendation for digitization of video signals (F_s = 13.5 MHz, YUV signals in 4:2:2 format).

CCIR-656 (ITU-R 656) – recommendation for interfacing CCIR-601 signals (most common variant: 8 bits parallel multiplexed YUV format).

CCITT – Comité Consultatif International du Télégraphe et du Téléphone (now ITU-T).

CIF – common intermediate format (360 × 288 @ 30 Hz).

CNR – carrier-to-noise ratio (or C/N) ratio (in dB) between the received power of the carrier and the noise power in the channel bandwidth.

COFDM – coded orthogonal frequency division multiplex (see OFDM).

CSA – common scrambling algorithm (scrambling algorithm specified by DVB).

CVBS – composite video baseband signal (colour composite video, e.g. NTSC, PAL or SECAM).

D1 – professional digital video recording format in component form (CCIR-656).

D2 – professional digital video recording format in composite form (NTSC, PAL or SECAM).

D2-MAC – duobinary multiplex analogue components (hybrid standard used on satellite and cable).

DAB – digital audio broadcasting (new European digital audio broadcasting standard).

DAC – digital-to-analogue converter (device converting a binary value into an analogue voltage or current).

DAVIC – digital audio visual council, a non-profit making association based in Geneva with members from all industries involved in digital technologies applied to audio and video, from content producer to service provider to hardware manufacturer. One of its goals is to define and specify open interfaces allowing maximal interoperability across countries, applications and services.

DBS – direct broadcast satellite (satellite in the 11.7–12.5 GHz band reserved for TV broadcast).

DC – direct current (coefficient of the null frequency in the DCT).

DCT – discrete cosine transform (temporal to frequency transform used in JPEG and MPEG).

DiSEqC® – digital satellite equipment control (control protocol allowing a bidirectional digital communication between the set-top box and the antenna for complex switching functions by modulating the 22 KHz tone with digital messages). Two versions (1.0 and 2.0) currently exist.

DPCM – differential pulse code modulation (coding of a value by its difference to the previous one).

DRAM – dynamic random access memory (read/write memory requiring a periodic refresh of the information, the most widespread due to its low cost).

DSM – digital storage medium (mass storage devices such as hard disk, tape or CD).

DSP – digital signal processor (processor specialized in processing of digitized analogue signals).

DTS – decoding time stamp (indicator of the decoding time of an MPEG access unit).

DVB – digital video broadcasting: European digital TV standard with three variants, DVB-C (cable), DVB-S (satellite), DVB-T (terrestrial).

DVB-CI – common interface (DVB interface for conditional access modules in PCMCIA form).

DVB-SI – system information (group of tables specified by DVB, additional to MPEG-2 PSI).

DVD – digital versatile disk (new unified format of laser disk with 4.7–19 Gbyte capacity).

E_b/N_o – ratio between the average bit energy E_b and noise density N_o (related to C/N).

EBU – European Broadcasting Union (French: Union Européenne de Radiodiffusion, UER). Organization grouping the main European broadcasters which, among other things, works on new broadcasting standards (ex: DAB, DVB) which are then approved by the ETSI.

ECM – entitlement control message (first type of conditional access message of the DVB standard).

EIT – event information table (optional table of DVB-SI indicating a new event).

ELG – European Launching Group (group at the origin of the DVB project in 1991).

EMM – entitlement management message (second type of conditional access message of the DVB standard).

EPG – electronic programme guide (graphical user interface for easier access to DVB programmes).

ES – elementary stream (output stream of an MPEG audio or video encoder).

ETSI – European Telecommunications Standards Institute (organization issuing the European standards in the field of telecommunications, ETS).

FCC – Federal Communications Commission (regulatory authority for telecommunications in the USA).

FEC – forward error correction (addition of redundancy to a digital signal before transmission, allowing errors to be corrected at the receiving end; synonym: channel coding).

FFT – fast Fourier transform (digital Fourier transform on sampled signals).

FIFO – first in, first out (type of memory often used as a buffer).

FSK – frequency shift keying (digital frequency modulation with two states).

FSS – fixed service satellite (satellite in the 10.7–11.7 GHz or 12.5–12.75 GHz bands originally reserved for telecommunications).

GOP – group of pictures (MPEG video layer: succession of pictures starting by an I picture).

H261 – compression standard used for ISDN videotelephony (bit-rate of $p \times 64$ kb/s).

HD-MAC – high definition MAC (high definition extension to the D2-MAC standard with 1250 lines).

HDTV – High Definition TeleVision (TV system with more than 1000 scanning lines).

I – in-phase; for QAM, designates the signal modulating the carrier following the 0° axis.

I – intra (picture); MPEG picture coded without reference to other pictures.

I^{2}C – inter-integrated circuits (serial interconnection bus between ICs developed by Philips).

I^{2}S – inter-integrated sound (serial link between digital sound ICs developed by Philips).

IDTV – Improved Definition TeleVision (TV system with a resolution between standard TV and HDTV).

IEC – International Electrotechnical Commission (international organization for standardization in the field of electrotechnics, electricity and electronics).

IEEE1284 – bidirectional high speed parallel interface (enhanced Centronics interface).

IEEE1394 – high speed serial interface (up to 400 Mb/s) which is the likely future standard for consumer digital *A/V* links (already used in some digital video recorders and camcorders).

IRD – integrated receiver decoder; popular synonym: set-top box.

ISI – inter-symbol interference (interference between successive symbols in a digital transmission).

ISO – International Standards Organization (international standardization organization within the UNO).

ITU – International Telecommunications Union (world regulation organization for telecommunications, previously CCITT).

JPEG – Joint Photographic Experts Group (standard for fixed pictures compression).

LNC – low noise converter (down-converter situated at the focus of a satellite antenna). Synonym = LNB (low noise block).

MP@ML – main profile at main level (main video format of the DVB standard).

MPEG – Motion Pictures Experts Group (group which developed the MPEG-1 and MPEG-2 standards, currently working on MPEG-4 for very low bit-rate compression).

MUSE – Japanese high definition television system (analogue system with digital assistance).

MUSICAM – masking universal sub-band integrated coding and multiplexing (coding process of MPEG-1 audio, layer 2 used by DAB and DVB).

NICAM – near instantaneous companded audio multiplexing (digital sound system for analogue TV using a QPSK modulated carrier at 5.85 or 6.55 MHz).

NIT – network information table (optional table of DVB-SI).

NTSC – National Television Standard Committee (colour TV system used in USA and most 60 Hz countries).

OFDM – orthogonal frequency division multiplex (digital modulation system based on a high number of carriers used for DAB and proposed for terrestrial DVB-T).

P – predictive (picture) MPEG picture coded with reference to the preceding I or P picture.

PAL – phase alternating line (colour TV system used in most European and 50 Hz countries).

PAT – program allocation table (DVB table indicating the PID of the components of a programme).

PCM – pulse code modulation (result of the digitization of an analogue signal).

PCMCIA (now renamed PC-Card) – Personal Computer Memory Card Association (designates the format used for PC extension modules and proposed by DVB for the detachable conditional access modules using the DVB-CI common interface).

PCR – program clock reference (information sent at regular intervals in MPEG-2 to synchronize the decoder's clock to the clock of the programme being decoded).

PES – packetized elementary stream (MPEG elementary stream after packetization).

PID – packet identifier (PES identification number in the DVB standard).

PMT – program map table (DVB table indicating the PID of the PAT of all programmes in a transport multiplex).

PRBS – pseudo-random binary sequence (used for signal scrambling).

PSI – program specific information (MPEG-2 mandatory tables: CAT, PAT, PMT).

PTS – presentation time stamp (information indicating the presentation time of a decoded image or sound).

PU – presentation unit (decoded picture or audio frame in MPEG).

Q – quadrature; for QAM, designates the signal modulating the carrier following the 90° axis.

QAM – quadrature amplitude modulation (modulation of two orthogonal derivates of a carrier by two signals).

QCIF – quarter common intermediate format (180 $\times$ 144 @ 15 Hz used for videotelephony).

QEF – quasi error-free (designates a channel with a BER $< 10^{-10}$).

QPSK – quadrature phase shift keying (phase modulation with four states, equivalent to 4-QAM).

RISC – reduced instruction set computer.

RLC – run length coding (data compression method exploiting repetitions).

RS(204, 188, 8) – abbreviated notation of the Reed–Solomon coding used by DVB.

RS232 – standardized asynchronous serial communication interface (relatively slow).

RST – running status table (optional table of DVB-SI informing on the current transmission).

SCR – system clock reference (information sent at regular intervals in MPEG-1 to synchronize the decoder's clock to the system clock).

SDRAM – synchronous dynamic random access memory (a new kind of high speed DRAM (16 bits organized) used with recent MPEG decoders).

SDT – service description table (optional table of DVB-SI).

SECAM – séquentiel couleur à mémoire (colour TV system mainly used in France and in eastern European countries).

SFN – single frequency network (terrestrial transmitter network using 8K OFDM modulation, allowing the same frequency band to be used for a large area).

SIF – source intermediate format (360 $\times$ 288 @ 25 Hz or 360 $\times$ 240 @ 30 Hz; basis for MPEG-1).

ST – stuffing table (optional table of DVB-SI).

STD – system target decoder (hypothetical reference decoder used in MPEG standards).

TDT – time and date table (optional table of DVB-SI).

TPS – transmission parameter signalling (modulation and channel coding parameters transmitted on pilot carriers of the OFDM multiplex in the DVB-T proposal).

VBS – video baseband signal (monochrome composite signal).

VLC – variable length coding (data compression method consisting of coding frequent elements with fewer bits than infrequent ones).

VLIW – very long instruction word (new type of processor using parallelism).

VSB – vestigial sideband (AM with one of the two sidebands truncated); used by all analogue TV standards and proposed for the terrestrial broadcasting of the digital 'Grand Alliance' US HDTV system (8 or 16-VSB).

WSS – wide screen signalling (signalling information on line 23 of the PAL+ signal, also used on standard PAL or SECAM, to indicate the format and other characteristics of the transmission).

Words and expressions

aliasing – disturbance caused by spectrum mixing when sampling a signal with a bandwidth exceeding half of the sampling frequency (during an A-to-D conversion, for instance).

asynchronous – in IEEE1394 terminology, designates the mode specified for the transport of non-time-critical data (used, for example, for function control or storage).

baseband – original frequency band of an analogue or digital signal before modulation or after demodulation.

block – in JPEG and MPEG this designates the portion of an 8 × 8 pixel picture to which the DCT is applied.

burst errors – multiple errors occurring in a short time with relatively long error-free periods in-between.

channel coding – addition of redundancy to a digital signal before transmission, allowing errors to be corrected at the receiving end (synonym: FEC).

comb filter – filter used in NTSC or PAL with 'teeth' corresponding to the stripes in the chrominance and luminance spectra for optimum separation of chrominance and luminance.

components video – colour video made of three elementary signals (e.g. RVB or YUV).

composite video – coded colour video using one signal only (NTSC, PAL or SECAM).

compression layer – in MPEG, designates the information at the output of the individual encoders (elementary streams, ESs).

constellation – simultaneous display in I/Q coordinates of the points representing all the possible states of a quadrature modulated signal (QAM, QPSK).

convolutional coding – 'inner' part of the channel coding for satellite and terrestrial transmissions, increasing the redundancy by providing two bitstreams from the original one; it corrects mainly random errors due to noise.

digitization – conversion of an analogue value into a (generally binary) number (synonym: analogue-to-digital conversion, ADC).

downlink – communication link from a satellite to earth station(s) or consumer receivers.

echo equalizer – device designed for cancellation or attenuation of the echoes introduced by transmission (cable transmission mainly).

encryption – encoding of information with a key to control its access.

energy dispersal – logic combination of a digital bitstream with a pseudo-random binary sequence (PRBS) to obtain an evenly distributed energy after modulation.

entropy coding – coding principle using variable length words to encode information elements depending on their probability of occurrence (synonym: variable length coding, VLC); the most well known method for VLC is the Huffmann algorithm.

Eurocrypt – conditional access system mainly used with the D2-MAC standard.

flash EPROM – non-volatile, electrically erasable and rewritable memory (in blocks).

flicker – disturbing periodic variation of the luminance of a picture when its refresh frequency is too low (below 50 Hz).

frame (audio) – elementary period during which the psycho-acoustical coding is performed (corresponds to 12 times 32 PCM samples); its duration varies from 8 to 12 ms depending on the sampling frequency.

granule – in MPEG audio (layer 2), designates a group of three consecutive sub-band samples (corresponds to 96 PCM samples).

interlaced scanning – scanning of a picture in two successive fields, one with odd lines and the other with even lines, in order to reduce by a factor of 2 the bandwidth required for a given resolution and a given refresh rate compared to a progressively scanned picture.

isochronous – in IEEE1394 terminology, designates the 'quasi-synchronous' mode used to transport time-critical data (real-time audio and video).

joint_stereo – MPEG audio mode exploiting the redundancy between left and right channels with two submodes (*MS_stereo*: coding of L + R and L − R; *intensity_stereo*: coding of common sub-band coefficients for high bands of L and R).

layer – in MPEG audio, defines the algorithm used for compression (there are three different layers).

layer – in MPEG video, corresponds to the hierarchical decomposition (from sequence to block).

letterbox – broadcast format used to transmit wide screen films (16/9 or more) on a standard 4/3 TV screen, leaving two horizontal black stripes at the top and bottom of the picture.

level – in MPEG-2, defines the spatial resolution of the picture to be coded.

line-locked clock – clock synchronized by a PLL loop to the line frequency of a video signal.

lossless compression – same as reversible coding (see this phrase; opposite: lossy compression).

lossy compression – compression process which discards some imperceptible or hardly perceptible information elements (opposite: lossless or reversible compression).

macroblock – picture area of 16×16 pixels used for motion estimation. A macroblock is made up of six blocks: 4 Y, 1 C_b and 1 C_r.

masking – occultation of the perception of a sound by a more powerful one at a near frequency (frequency masking) and/or time (temporal masking).

motion estimation – determination of a motion vector allowing an area of a picture to be deduced from an area from a previous picture.

multicrypt – one of the conditional access options in DVB, based on a detachable CA module connected via the 'common interface' DVB-CI.

node – in IEEE1394 terminology, designates a participant connected to the bus.

orthogonal sampling – sampling of a video signal by means of a clock locked to the line frequency in order to obtain samples with fixed positions on a rectangular grid.

orthogonality – property of a digitally modulated multiple carrier system when the spacing between consecutive carriers is equal to the inverse of the period of the modulating signal, so that the spectrum of any carrier presents zeroes for the central value of the neighbouring carriers (OFDM modulation).

padding – non-significant bits added to adjust the duration of an audio frame (padding bits), or non-significant stream added to adjust the bit-rate of a bitstream (padding stream).

payload – for MPEG-2 transport packets (188 bytes), this designates the 'useful' 184 bytes following the header.

peritel – 21 pin audio/video connector (also known as SCART plug or EUROCONNECTOR) used to interconnect audiovisual equipment (TV, VCR, set-top box, etc.).

pixel (or pel) abbreviation of 'picture element' – the smallest element of an imaging or display device. In digital TV, it corresponds to the visual representation of one sample of a digitized picture.

profile – in MPEG-2, defines the toolbox used for video encoding.

progressive scanning – scanning of all the lines of a picture in numerical order in only one frame containing all picture lines (type of scanning used for computer monitors).

psycho-acoustic model – mathematical model of the behaviour of the human auditive system, based, among other things, on the frequency and temporal masking effects.

puncture – operation consisting of taking only a part of the bits generated by the convolutional coding to reduce its redundancy, at the expense of a reduced robustness (used in DVB-S and DVB-T).

quantization – measurement of a quantity with a limited number of discrete values (distant from the quantization step), for instance in an analogue-to-digital conversion or a compression process.

quantization noise – noise introduced by an analogue-to-digital conversion process, mainly due to the uncertainty on the least significant bit (representing the quantization step).

Reed–Solomon coding – outer part of the DVB channel coding, which adds 16 parity bytes to the 188 byte packets and allows correction of up to 8 bytes per packet; it is denoted RS (204, 188, 8).

reversible coding – coding allowing the recovery of the exact original information by applying the reverse process (synonym: lossless coding; opposite: lossy coding).

roll-off factor – characteristic of the steepness of the filtering applied to a digital signal in order to limit its bandwidth, generally with a view to modulation.

sampling – periodic acquisition of the value of an analogue signal, generally with a view to converting it into a digital number.

scalable profile – MPEG-2 profile allowing different levels of quality to be obtained from the same bitstream (in terms of resolution for *spatially scalable profiles* or signal-to-noise ratio for *SNR scalable profiles*).

scaling factor – in MPEG audio, a 6 bit multiplying factor applied to each sub-band coefficient for the duration of a frame (giving a 128 dB range with 64 values in steps of 2 dB).

sequence – in MPEG, an uninterrupted series of GOP defined with the same basic parameters.

set-top box – popular denomination of an integrated receiver decoder (IRD).

simulcast – simultaneous transmission of a programme in two or more standards (e.g. PAL and DVB), generally during a transition period between these standards.

simulcrypt – principle consisting of sending ECM and EMM for more than one conditional access system for one programme, in order to allow reception by different types of decoder.

slice – in MPEG, a slice is a portion of the picture made up of horizontally consecutive macroblocks (most of the time a complete row). It is used for intra-frame addressing and resynchronization.

source coding – ensemble of coding operations aiming to reduce the quantity of information delivered by a source (synonym: compression).

spectral efficiency – ratio (in bits/s per Hz) between the bit-rate of a bitstream and the bandwidth occupied by the RF signal modulated by this bitstream.

square pixels – name given to the pixels obtained when sampling results in an equivalent resolution along the two axes of the picture (e.g. 640 × 480 for a 4/3 picture).

sub-band sample – in MPEG audio, output signal of one of the 32 sub-band filters (duration: 32 PCM samples, corresponding to 1 ms at 32 kHz sampling rate).

symbol – in a digital transmission, this is the modulating information element. The number of bits/symbol depends on the modulation type (e.g. 2 bits/symbol for QPSK, 6 for 64-QAM).

symbol rate – number of symbols transmitted per second.

system layer – in MPEG-1, designates the form of the packetized information after multiplexing.

table (MPEG-2 PSI and DVB-SI) – descriptive information necessary to access DVB transmissions or making this access easier.

thresholding – elimination of values below a given threshold (used in video compression to reduce the amount of information to be transmitted).

transponder – electronic device in a communication satellite receiving information from an earth station and re-sending it after frequency conversion and amplification to earth station(s) or consumers; there is generally one transponder per RF channel.

transport packet – packet of 188 bytes (4 header bytes + 184 payload bytes) forming the elementary blocks of an MPEG-2 transport bitstream to which the error correction is applied.

uplink – communication link from an earth station to a satellite, supplying the information to be rebroadcast by one or more transponder(s).

Bibliography

Books

Bic, J.C., Duponteil, D., Imbeaux, J.C. 1991: *Elements of digital communication*. Paris: Wiley (in English).

Brémaud, P. 1995: *Signal et communications*. Paris: Ellipses (in French).

Chambers, W.G. 1985: *Basics of communication and coding*. Oxford: Clarendon Press (in English).

Cohen, G., Dornstetter, J.L., Godlewski, P. 1992: *Codes correcteurs d'erreur*.
Paris: Masson (in French).

Hill, R. 1986: *A first course in coding theory*. Oxford: Clarendon Press (in
English).

Moreau, N. 1995: *Techniques de compression des signaux*. Paris: Masson (in
French).

Petersen, D. 1992: *Audio, video and data telecommunications*. London:
McGraw-Hill (in English).

Poli, A., Huguet, L. 1989: *Codes correcteurs*. Paris: Masson (in French).

Reimers, U., Fechter, F., Jaeger, D., Johansen, C., Ladebusch, U., Ricken, C., Roy,
A., Verse, A. 1995: *Digitales Fernsehtechnik*. Berlin: Springer (in German).

Sandbank, C.P. 1990: *Digital Television*. Chichester: Wiley.

Viterbi, A.J., Omura, J.K. 1979: *Principals of digital communication and coding*. New York: McGraw Hill (in English).

Ziemer, A., *et al.* 1994: *Digitales Fernsehen*. Heidelberg: R. von Decker (in
German).

Official documents (in English)

BT 601 (ITU-R) Studio encoding parameters of digital television for standard 4:
3 and wide screen 16:9 aspect ratios (Recommendation CCIR-601).

BT 656 (ITU-R) Interfaces for digital component video signals in 525 line and 625 line television systems operating at the 4:2:2 level of Rec. 601 (Recommendation CCIR-656).

ETR154 (ETSI/EBU) Implementation guidelines for the use of MPEG-2 systems, audio and video in satellite and cable broadcasting applications.

ETR162 (ETSI/EBU) Allocation of SI codes for DVB systems.

ETS 300 421 (ETSI/EBU) Framing structure channel coding and modulation for satellite services.

ETS 300 429 (ETSI/EBU) Framing structure channel coding and modulation for cable services.

ETS 300 468 (ETSI/EBU) Specification for Service Information (SI) in DVB systems.

ETS 300 472 (ETSI/EBU) Specification for conveying ITU-R system B Teletext in DVB bitstreams.

ETS 300 748 (ETSI/EBU) Framing structure, channel coding and modulation for Multipoint Video Distribution Systems (MVDS) at 10 GHz and above (based on ETS 300 421 DVB-S).

IEEE1394, 1995: Standard for a high performance serial bus.

ISO 10918 (ISO/IEC) Digital compression and coding of continuous tone still images (JPEG).

ISO 11172-1, 11172-2, 11172-3 (ISO/IEC) Coding of moving pictures and associated audio for digital storage media up to about 1.5 Mb/s (MPEG-1 system, video, audio).

ISO 13818-1, 13818-2, 13818-3 (ISO/IEC) Coding of moving pictures and associated audio (MPEG-2 system, video, audio).

prETS 300 744 (ETSI/EBU) Framing structure channel coding and modulation for terrestrial services (in final phase of standardization).

prETS 300 749 (ETSI/EBU, draft) Framing structure, channel coding and modulation for MMDS systems below 10 GHz (based on ETS 300 429, DVB-C).

Some useful Internet addresses

ASTRA:	http://www.astra.lu
DVB:	http://www.dvb.org
EBU (UER):	http://www.ebu.ch
ETSI:	http://www.etsi.fr
EUTELSAT:	http://www.eutelsat.org
IEC (CEI):	http://www.iec.org
IEEE:	http://www.ieee.org
ISO:	http://www.iso.ch

Index